Tangible
press

VIEW FROM THE BOTTOM

50 Years of Bass Playing with
Bob Dylan, The Doors,
Miles Davis and Everybody Else

by HARVEY BROOKS

with FRANK BEACHAM and BONNIE BROOKS

View from the Bottom

© 2020 by Harvey Brooks
with Frank Beacham and Bonnie Brooks

Tangible Press is a wholly owned and operated Subdivision of Punk Hart Productions LLC

Cover design by John Howells

Printed in the United States of America
First Printing, 2020

ISBN: 1-7334579-5-X
ISBN-13: 978-1-7334579-5-8

Library of Congress Control Number: 2020905149

This book is dedicated to Bonnie Ruza Brooks, the love of my life and keeper of my soul.

Acknowledgements

I most of all want to thank the love of my life Bonnie Brooks, my best friend, wife of 31 years, partner and the sole reason this memoir has come to life. She has pulled lost memories out from beyond and edited my gibberish into clarity. She filled the gaps when I spaced out and added what was needed to continue the story, never letting me settle for less.

I want to thank Frank Beacham for his organization and meticulous attention to detail, his interviews, quotes from artists, music business people and transcriptions of our Jerusalem to Manhattan conversations. Thanks, Frank!

Special thanks to family and friends for helping me bring this project to fruition.....Chris and Sally Larsen, Matt Adams, Jim Motavalli and Jeff Michels.

Thank you: Donald Fagen, Bonnie Raitt, John Sebastian, John Densmore, Vinnie Pastore, Steve Berkowitz, Brian Ray, Michael Lang and the others who shared their memories for this book. I believe that truly talented people inspire others to realize greatness within themselves. Distinguished bassists such as Charles Mingus, Scott LaFaro, Ron Carter, James Jamerson, Chuck Rainey and Duck Dunn are such musicians for me.

Foreword

Maybe you never heard of Harvey Brooks. But if you love music, believe me, you've heard Harvey Brooks.

Harvey is one of the greatest electric bass guitar players ever, a musician's musician. For decades, starting in the 60s, he worked with everybody from Bob Dylan to Miles Davis to Jimi Hendrix to the Doors to Joni Mitchell, and so many more. His bass lines are the foundation of much of the iconic rock, blues and jazz music of that amazing era.

Time and again, when something big, something different, something new was happening on the music scene, Harvey was there. He saw everything; he knew, gigged with and hung out with everybody. He had enough wild, weird and wonderful experiences for several lifetimes, including — to pick one of many stories — a long night of partying in New York City that wound up involving Hendrix, Jim Morrison, Janis Joplin and Tiny Tim.

The best part is, Harvey remembers it all, and he recounts it vividly in this book, which takes the reader on a riveting journey from his early days on the Lower East Side, through the wild music scene of the Sixties and Seventies, and ultimately to his current life in, of all places, Jerusalem, where he's still making music. En route, he reflects on the life lessons he learned — mostly the hard way — and shares insights into his musical craft.

I was lucky enough to have seen Harvey perform back when I

was a blues-obsessed college student in the Sixties. He was a legend even then, for his sound, his bass lines, his calm and steady stage presence. A few decades later, I was even luckier: I actually got to perform with Harvey. I played guitar in the Rock Bottom Remainders, a now semi-retired band that was made up mostly of authors, including, at the time, Stephen King, Amy Tan, Ridley Pearson, Roy Blount, Jr., Barbara Kingsolver, Kathi Goldmark and Matt Groening. We were a bad band, but we had a lot of fun.

Our original music director was Al Kooper, whom Harvey has known forever. In the early 90s, Al was doing a gig at the now-defunct Bottom Line in New York. As a goof, he wanted me to do a song, specifically Van Morrison's classic three-chord garage-band rocker "Gloria." I played guitar, and somehow Al convinced Harvey to play bass. This was like asking Michelangelo to paint a garage, but Harvey cheerfully agreed.

And thus it was that I got to play "Gloria" with Harvey Freaking Brooks. It was one of the musical highlights of my life, although I note that somehow Harvey failed to mention that particular performance in this book.

But everything else is in here. It's a fascinating story, a long strange trip with a happy ending. And Harvey Brooks, as you'll see when you turn the page, is as good a storyteller as he is a musician.

Dave Barry

Introduction

My name is Harvey Brooks. I was in the right place at the right time. For the past 50 years, I have played electric bass guitar contributing to some of the quintessential pop, blues and jazz recordings of the musical revolution that began in the 1960s. How I got there and my experiences along the way are the subject of this book.

It has taken more than three years to put to paper my *View from the Bottom*. Here I share particular times and places to help the reader understand my life and the forces that shape my art and musicianship. Traveling many paths and working with a wide variety of well-known musicians, I have been most fortunate in my quest.

As a session player, I've recorded with Bob Dylan (*Highway 61 Revisited* and *New Morning*), Miles Davis (*Bitches Brew* and *Big Fun*), The Fabulous Thunderbirds (*Roll of the Dice*), Richie Havens (*Mixed Bag*), The Doors (*The Soft Parade*), Seals and Crofts (*Summer Breeze* and *Down Home*), Cass Elliot (*Dream A Little Dream*), John Sebastian (*John B. Sebastian*), Al Kooper (*Super Session*), Mike Bloomfield (*The Electric Flag*) and Karen Dalton (*In My Own Time*). I've also recorded with Peter, Paul and Mary, Tom Rush, Eric Andersen, Judy Collins, Jimi Hendrix, Loudon Wainwright III, John Cale, John Simon, Fontella Bass and Mavis Staples.

I have performed live with Bob Dylan at Forest Hills and the Hollywood Bowl and with The Electric Flag at the 1967 Monterey Pop Festival. Add to that The Doors at Madison Square Garden in New York City and the Forum in Los Angeles, as well as Jimi Hendrix, Richie Havens and Donald Fagen's Rock 'N' Soul tour,

11

featuring Michael McDonald, Boz Skaggs and Phoebe Snow. In addition, there's the Paul Butterfield Blues Band, Clarence Clemons and the Red Bank Rockers and The Rekooperators with Al Kooper. I've had rich, life-defining experiences with them all.

I started my producing career at Columbia Records producing albums for John Hall and Bobby Lester. Independently, I produced Quicksilver Messenger Service with Nick Gravenites for Capitol Records and Karen Dalton's *In My Own Time* for Just Sunshine Records. I co-produced The Electric Flag's second album with John Simon and wrote the liner notes.

I was born in Manhattan and grew up in Queens, which is where I was living when — thanks to my sister Roberta — I first heard black rhythm and blues. There was a feel to the music and an exciting church-derived soulful sound in the rhythm and harmony. I didn't understand what it was all about at the time, but I knew it was very exciting and felt good. Little did I realize that the sound would have a substantial impact on the music I would play in the future and my accomplishments in the music business. This is the beginning of my story.

Early Life

I was encouraged by my parents who chose to accept my artistic whims.

High School Guitar Lessons with Jerry Oddo. (me on the left)

Pop in the Phillippines during World War II

Mom relaxing at a bungalow colony in Monticello, NY 1948

Mom and me

Bonnie Ruza 1962

Me (third row right) with my Little League team
coached by my father (top left)

My sister Bert and me at the beach

My sister Bert

Me and brother Gary   My High School Graduation

Brother Gary and me

CHAPTER 1

I Started Out as a Child

I was born on July 4. I am the third of four children born to Fay and Sam Goldstein. My parents were children of immigrants who lived on the lower Eastside. Frank and Becky Goldstein and Louis and Sarah Poland had emigrated from Poland to the United States in about 1900.

My older brother, Nathan (Natey), died before I was born. He was five and a half years old when he got off a bus coming home from school. Not waiting for my Grandma Sarah to meet him, he crossed the street and was killed by a truck that drove through a red light. I only knew him from a picture my mother showed me of him sitting on a pony that hung on our wall.

My father was a truck driver and my mother, who never learned to drive, was a stay-at-home mom. Mom was a real pioneer. In 1951, when I was seven, she moved us out to the country, or what we considered the country, Bell Park Manor-Terrace in Queens Village, Queens, a development built for Jewish World War II veterans. It was in New York City, but to us it was *the country*. Trees, horses, ponds for fishing and skating, open spaces, dirt roads and no high-rise buildings.

We had a two-bedroom upstairs apartment with one bathroom. My Grandma Sarah lived with us. My parents slept in the living room. I shared my older sister's bedroom and Grandma had her own room. I was ten years old when my brother Gary was born in 1954.

I was seven years old when we moved in and over the next few years did what kids did then, playing stick and punch ball, made go carts with orange crates, 2 x 4s, wheels and axles from baby carriages left in basement storage rooms, and rode bikes with playing cards or baseball cards attached to the wheel spokes with clothes pins.

My Dad was a baseball aficionado, a New York Yankee hardcore fan and I was close behind. In 1952, Topps put out their first set of bubble gum cards and we kids spent every nickel we could get our hands on to buy them. Mickey Mantle, Duke Snyder and Willie Mays were the local heroes representing the NY Yankees, the Brooklyn Dodgers and the New York Giants.

Collecting cards for us was not about their value as collectibles. We were in it purely to have complete sets, our favorite players and would trade, flip or toss cards against a wall to get them. I remember one particular episode with Mark Kaplan, a kid who lived across the street. Behind my two-story apartment building was our storage and a laundry room. There was a ramp with steps in the middle that declined on an angle to a flat bottom cement floor with a wall in front and to the left, two doors on the right leading to the rooms. This was our baseball card playing field.

We would flip and toss cards maybe twenty at a time and whoever owned the card closest to wall would win all the cards. This one time, Mark brought out his many Mickey Mantles and his whole Yankees collection. I wiped him out. I guess the cards were just going my way. He started to cry when he realized what had just happened. His whole collection was in my shoebox. I returned most of his cards the next day. I would rather have a friend to play with than just cards.

Around that time, my sister Roberta got me interested in music through her love of singing. She would take me to see the Alan Freed shows at the Brooklyn Paramount that usually had 10 to 15 acts plus the Red Prysock/Sam "The Man" Taylor/Al Sears Big Band. We also went to the shows put on by DJ Murray the K at the Brooklyn Fox.

We would get up at 5:30 in the morning to take the bus and train into Brooklyn and grab up-front seats. There were three or four shows a day. So, whether it was good or bad weather we were in the front of the line that was always around the block. When we got in we'd get as close as we could. I didn't know much about this R&B music, but I knew it made me feel good.

JHS 109 was a typical public school filled with students having only one thing in common, which was having to be there. In junior high, I saw myself as a chubby, cross-eyed kid with many insecurities. My French teacher Mr. Iorio had a weekly show and tell class. My friend Bob Rose brought in his guitar and played for the class. I was hooked!

Bob taught me two chords and asked me to play a church party two weeks later. That was my first gig. I made fifty cents. Next came our band The Citations, consisting of Bob Rose on lead and me on rhythm guitar, Teddy Josephs on drums and Lenny on sax.

My parents were very supportive without being pushy. The guitar they bought me was a steel string, brand name *Stella*. They found me a guitar teacher. His name was Jerry Oddo and was the inventor of the tricky pick, which is a double-serated-on-one-edge pick held together by a thin rubber washer. Hard to find now.

I wasn't allowed to practice in the living room, only in my bedroom. After I got my first fake book and could play some songs, I was allowed to bring the guitar out and my Father would sing tunes like "That Old Gang of Mine" and "Sunny Side of the Street" with me playing along.

Playing the guitar gave me my first glimpse at the world outside my two-bedroom family apartment. I wanted to get a better guitar as I began to improve. My parents said that I would need to get a job to pay for it. This was my first realization that parents didn't pay for everything all the time. They suggested I get a paper route. You could earn enough money if your service is good and your customers will tip you well. They were right!

I spent many cold and snowy late afternoons standing in doorways waiting to collect my money hearing Dick Clark's American Bandstand in the background. It took one winter and a Chanukah, Christmas holiday for me to buy a new Harmony Monterey Grand Auditorium Arched guitar.

In my freshman year at Martin Van Buren High School, I joined a high school fraternity named Sigma Alpha Rho (SAR). High school fraternities and sororities were basically social clubs for people who liked each other and had some common bonds or interests.

At one of the fraternity meetings that took place in the home of brothers Lloyd and Morey Ruza I met SAR alumni Sid Davidoff, a few years older than me, and unbeknownst to me my future wife, Bonnie. Sid was involved in politics and had aspirations which were way above my pay scale. At that time, I had a band with my friend Bob Rose called The Citations. After the meeting ended, Sid recruited The Citations to play at some political functions and became the Citations' manager.

Davidoff eventually became New York Mayor John Lindsay's right-hand man/administrative assistant and more importantly, was the guiding force in my transition from guitar to bass. He said, "The group needs a bass. They have these electric ones. I'll get you one and you'll try it." He got me a Tower electric bass, made in Japan. One evening after rehearsal Davidoff took us down to Trude Heller's, one of the hip music clubs in Greenwich Village to hear the bass player with The Four Saints. He was great and I was sold on my new position.

The Citations played local dances, Jewish centers and church functions in competition with other local bands such as the Rockin' Chairs and Al Kooper's Aristocats. Eric Krakow was the bass player in the Aristocats. He lived in the same development in Queens as I did and we were friends. Before he left for dental school, he introduced me to Al, who was also a neighborhood guy.

Upon graduating high school, I began a BA program at Queens College. Simultaneously I played six nights a week at such clubs as Trude Heller's, The Eighth Wonder, Wagon Wheel and The Peppermint Lounge in Greenwich Village. The constant playing meant I slept through a lot of classes, and I dropped out of Queens College in 1963 to play music full time.

At one of these clubs I met Carmine "Wassel" DeNoia, who said he was the manager of R&B singer Freddie Scott. Freddie had a hit with "Hey Girl," written by Gerry Goffin and Carole King, and was later signed to Bert Berns' Shout label. Wassal wanted to recruit a backup band for record promotion gigs, or record hops as they were called at that time.

Wassel seemed to be the kind of guy you wanted to have on your side. So I joined up with my buddy Al Kooper. Our first gig was in Boston. The club was located in Roxbury in the heart of the African-American community, circa 1963.

We pulled into the club. Idris Muhammad (Leo Morris at that time) was playing drums. We did two shows. We finished about 1:30 a.m. and went to the Hooker Haven Hotel (my name for this seedy dive) on Washington Street. Idris and I were roommates. There was activity in the hallway all night long and our room door had little peepholes. What a gig!

The next gig was a record hop in Brooklyn at the Lion's Club with Freddy Scott. We were all sitting in the lounge waiting for our turn to perform when the pay phone rang. Wassal picked it up, and that's how we learned that Sam Cooke had died.

Sam Cooke was the representative of church R&B soul music to me. "You Send Me" and "A Change is Gonna Come" set the bar for crossing the segregationist lines for 1960s pop music. Sam was a personal friend of Freddie Scott's and for me it was like losing a friend. Through his music he made me feel good and I would look forward to his next new song.

I was invited to meet the Exciters' record label owner, Roulette Records' Morris Levy. It was like walking into an episode of *The Sopranos*. Levy owned many companies and night clubs, including the jazz club Birdland. Morris said, pointing to me, "This guy awright?" Wassel shrugged, which I suppose meant I was OK. Levy was widely known for falsely taking writing credit in order to receive royalties — enriching himself at the expense of many of his signed artists, especially black R&B artists.

The Exciters at that time were Herb Rooney, Brenda Reid, Carolyn Johnson and Lillian Walker, plus the Jolly Green Giants backup band, which included me.

A year later, in the winter of 1963, I was 19 years old on my first professional tour. The Exciters, who'd had a hit called "Tell Him" in 1962, toured the east coast from New York's Brooklyn Apollo to Bangor, Maine in Herb Rooney's 1963 Oldsmobile 88 with Herb driving and Brenda navigating in the front seat and Carolyn, Lillian and me scrunched together in the back, trying to stay warm as we drove through blizzards. The hotels were basic and even had heat sometimes. The menu was mostly Howard Johnson specials, but it was the real deal. I couldn't have gone to a better school than Exciters 101, and the people couldn't have been nicer to me.

"Tell Him" had faded on the pop charts, and we were out promoting "Do Wah Diddy Diddy," their next release. But Manfred Mann covered it over in England and had a huge international hit, cancelling out The Exciters' version.

When the tour was over it was time for me to move on. I loved working with The Exciters, who were great performers. It was always fun, even when traveling and staying in depressing cheap hotels. That kind of thing was always forgotten at showtime.

In 1964, the Borough of Queens hosted the World's Fair. This "universal and international" exposition had as a theme "Peace Through Understanding," dedicated to "Man's Achievement on a Shrinking Globe in an Expanding Universe." The message was symbolized by a 12-story high, stainless steel model of the earth called the Unisphere. It's still there in Flushing Meadows-Corona Park, having been fully restored in 1994.

The fair ran for two six-month seasons, April 22 to October 18, 1964 and April 21 to October 17, 1965, and is best remembered as a showcase of mid-20th-century American culture and technology. More than 51 million people attended the fair, though less than the hoped-for 70 million. It remains a touchstone for New York–area Baby Boomers who visited the optimistic fair as children before the turbulent years of civil rights, the Vietnam War, and a host of cultural changes.

I knew the guy who had the ice cream concession in Carousel Park, one of the Fair's venues. They needed a band to alternate sets with the carousel and asked if I could put one together. Kooper and I had been practicing with a singer and drummer to play some gigs, so the timing couldn't have been better.

The bandstand stood opposite the carousel about 25 feet off the ground and open to the night air. No matter the weather, just like the postman, The Clubmen delivered. The band featured Al Kooper on his Vinnie Bell guitar, Bobby Mariko on vocals, Joey Michaels on drums and me on bass.

As soon as the Carousel stopped rotating the stage lights lit up and the Clubmen started playing, rain or shine. Our repertoire consisted of British Invasion stuff from the Kinks, Rolling Stones and the Beatles, but we also did the Isley Brothers and Wilson Pickett, with whom I'd have a memorable run-in later.

Little did I know at the time that this gig would lead to me being invited to play on Bob Dylan's *Highway 61 Revisited* album, and then to tour with him.

CHAPTER 2

The Highway 61 Sessions

1965: The first U.S. combat troops arrive in Vietnam. By the end of the year, 190,000 American soldiers are in Southeast Asia.

It was July 28, 1965. I was playing a gig with Chico Holiday's trio at the Sniffin Court Inn on East 36th Street in Manhattan. During a break, I went next door to my usual hangout between sets, the Burger Heaven, where I got a phone call from my friend, Al Kooper. "Can you play bass tomorrow on a recording session with Bob Dylan?" I responded, "Who is Bob Dylan?"

Al filled me in, and without thinking about it I took the gig. The next morning after my morning coffee, I drove from my parents' house in Queens on the Long Island Expressway through the midtown tunnel to Manhattan in my recently acquired 1965 Ford Mustang 2+2. I parked in the indoor garage on 54th Street and crossed over to 799 Seventh Avenue. I walked about 15 feet into the lobby and took the elevator to the seventh floor, where Columbia Studio A was located. It was there that I would record Bob Dylan's *Highway 61 Revisited* album and my new reality would begin.

I opened the door to the control room, took a deep breath and entered. A thin, frizzy-haired guy dressed in Levi jeans and boots was standing in the front of the mixing console listening to a play-back of what turned out to be "Like a Rolling Stone." I assumed this was Bob Dylan. I spotted Kooper walking toward me from the back of the control room and introductions were made. Dylan affirmed my existence and went back to his listening. Al then walked me around the control room to meet the producer, Bob Johnston, and Albert Grossman, Bob's manager. Grossman was a Ben Franklin look-alike who had a long gray ponytail and wore round wire-rimmed glasses. With introductions over, it was time to set-up. I walked into the studio, plugged into an Ampeg B-15 bass amp and began to tune.

Though I was only 21, I had already been on tour and had performed with many R&B acts, which included playing the Brooklyn Apollo with Chuck Jackson, Baby Washington and the Exciters. I had worked with varying styles and felt I could adapt to about anything on the fly. For that reason, I was looking forward to any musical challenge this guy Bob Dylan would throw my way.

Abruptly, the studio door burst open and in stormed guitarist Michael Bloomfield, an intense spark of pure energy. He was wearing penny loafers, jeans and a white shirt with rolled-up sleeves. He had a Fender Telecaster hanging over his shoulder that was wet from the rain he had encountered on the way over. His sincere smile was electric and friendly. Though it was the first time we had met, I felt instantly simpatico with him.

The other players on the session included Bobby Gregg on drums, Paul Griffin and Frank Owens on piano and Al on organ — the first time he played that instrument. At the first session, Joe

Macho Jr. or Russ Savakus had played bass, but Dylan wanted a more sympathetic feel for the rest of the sessions. He was looking for a bass player whom he didn't have to think about and felt comfortable with. Al knew I was a good choice, which is why he recommended me to Dylan.

In talking to Bob, I admitted to him that I hadn't heard any of his music before the session but was very impressed with "Like a Rolling Stone," which I heard when I walked into the studio. "Well, these songs are a little different," Bob responded. I assumed he meant from his past work, but Bob was bit vague. He gave me a kind of crooked smile and then lit up a cigarette.

Tom Wilson, who had produced the session that included "Like a Rolling Stone" a couple of weeks earlier, was replaced for unknown reasons. The new producer was Bob Johnston, a Columbia staff producer from Nashville who was already producing Patti Page when he got the Dylan assignment.

Johnston had a documentary-style "keep the tape rolling" approach to producing, which allowed him to capture a live feeling and special moments that happen between takes in the studio. He was frustrated by the technical bureaucracy at Columbia and ordered several tape machines brought into the control room, so he could keep one running at all times in order to capture anything Dylan might want to keep. This tactic worked quite well for both Bobs.

Though the first session for *Highway 61 Revisited* had been recorded two weeks earlier, a lot had happened in the interim. "Like a Rolling Stone," recorded at the first session, had been released and took off. Four days earlier, Dylan had been booed by the crowd when he had gone electric with the Paul Butterfield Blues Band at the Newport Folk Festival. It was a pivotal time in his career. He was in the transition from being a "pure" folk artist to becoming a rock and roll legend.

Here I was at the second session, uncertain and waiting to hear what was on Bob's mind. In a few minutes, he came out of the control room. Johnston had set up three-sided baffles, leaving the side that faced the band open so we could see him. Bob sang "Tombstone Blues" a few times with just his guitar as accompaniment.

There were no chord charts for anyone. It was all done by ear. As a habit, I made a few quick chord charts for myself as I listened to him perform the song. Everyone focused on Bob, watching for every nuance. Then, the band went for it. As we began recording, Bob was still working on the lyrics. He was constantly editing as we were recording. I thought it was an amazing way that he worked. His guitar or piano part was the guiding element through each song. Every musician in that room had their eyes and ears glued to him, yet his poker face never revealed what he was thinking.

"Tombstone Blues" was my introduction to Mike Bloomfield's guitar playing, and I was blown away by his choices. Before we started playing, we were talking about what might happen. His comment was, "I have no idea, but when he's not singing I'm gonna fill." Dylan — like Miles Davis — didn't want to talk about what to play. He wanted his best performance to determine the master take. I figured I better find something that works before he does so I can be there with him on the final.

It might have taken a couple of takes for everyone to lock in. There were mistakes, of course, but they didn't matter. If the feel was there and the performance was successful, that's all he cared about. In real life, that's the way it is. If the overall performance happens, it's a keeper. Bob would go into the control room and listen. Bob Johnston may have been the producer keeping the tape rolling, but it was all Bob Dylan deciding what felt right and what didn't.

As we played, I quickly learned about the different members of the band. Bobby Gregg was a very good, straight-ahead studio drummer. He was the kind of player who dictated a bass drum pattern for the bass player and set up the rhythmic pattern of the song and keeping the tempo relaxed.

The phrasing of Dylan and Bloomfield was very sympathetic. An explosive player, Bloomfield was aggressive and played a little bit in front of the beat on rhythm parts. My goal was to find a bass line that would help the groove happen. Bob set the feel and direction with his rhythm and my bass parts reflected what I got from the rhythm guitar or piano and Bobby Gregg's drums. It was necessary for me to play simple and solid so that all the energy coming from Bloomfield was maintained. If everybody were to rush, the tempo would be fluctuating back and forth.

Dylan loved Michael, who was a unique guitar player. He was not your relaxed, in-the-pocket groove guy. He went for it all the time.

Most of my previous playing experience had been in R&B bands that performed tunes by Wilson Pickett, Jackie Wilson, the Beatles and the Rolling Stones. Playing with Bob Dylan was much more personal because he was writing new songs about people and events.

"Positively Fourth Street" was issued as a single-only release, the follow-up to "Like A Rolling Stone." It became his third-best-selling single. We were all sitting in the studio feeling relaxed when Bob started playing. As he played and sang the lyric I started to work out my part but kept being drawn back to listening to the lyric. The chord changes were great but that lyric.

After we recorded it, I sat down in the control room and really listened. This was not a love song. This was not "Kumbaya." Dylan was telling somebody off in no uncertain terms.

I wish that for just one time you could stand inside my shoes
And just for that one moment I could be you

Yes, I wish that for just one time you could stand inside my shoes
You'd know what a drag it is to see you

OUCH!!

At the close of the session that first night, Bob attempted to record "Desolation Row," accompanied only by Al on electric guitar and me on bass. There was no drummer, as Bobby Gregg had already gone home. This electric version was eventually released in 2005 on *The Bootleg Series Vol. 7* album.

Bob Johnston

Bob Johnston had a love of and even a bias toward Nashville musicians. It became an underlying topic the entire session about how great they were. He kept talking about how cool Nashville is. With his repeated comments, I felt it was bit disparaging towards us. It seemed that Johnston thought of us as New York bumpkins. I thought he was stiff. His Nashville bias played into which version of "Desolation Row" was used. In my opinion the version without drums that Al and I had done that night was slower and definitely more soulful. Clearly, Johnston thought otherwise. On August 2, five more takes were done on "Desolation Row"!

The version of the song ultimately used on the album was recorded at an overdub session on August 4. This time, Johnston's personal friend, Nashville guitarist Charlie McCoy — a great player — was visiting New York City and was invited to contribute an improvised acoustic guitar part. Russ Savakus played bass.

Johnston's love of Nashville would eventually take him there. After a couple of years in New York City, he became head of Columbia Records in Nashville. He finally joined the session musicians that he liked so much. After our album, Johnston's relationship with Dylan was cemented. He went on to produce Dylan's *Blonde on Blonde* in 1966, *John Wesley Harding* in 1967, *Nashville Skyline* in 1969 and both *Self Portrait* and the second Dylan album I played on, *New Morning*, in 1970.

When I left the studio after the final *Highway 61* session, I didn't have any sense of whether or not we had created a hit record. I did know, however, that all the songs felt good. They felt solid. I now understand why *Highway 61 Revisited* was such a successful record. Bob got it. He has an amazing talent and knows what he wants. When he got what he wanted, he'd say, "That's it...next." Occasionally, someone would suggest trying another take. But most of the time Bob was in control.

In looking back, by calling me into that session my childhood friend Al Kuperschmid/Kooper gave me a definite step up into my new career as a studio musician.

CHAPTER 3

On the Road with Bob Dylan

1965: Rev. Martin Luther King, Jr. and more than 2,600 others are arrested in Selma, Alabama during demonstrations against voter-registration rules.

After recording *Highway 61 Revisited*, I got a call from Albert Grossman, Dylan's manager, asking that I drop by his Manhattan office to sign some papers and talk. When I got there, Albert wanted to know what I thought of Dylan and was I available for more work with him. He told me that Bob liked my playing and wanted me to perform at a couple of concerts with him — one on August 28 at the Forest Hills Tennis Stadium in Queens and the other at the Hollywood Bowl in Los Angeles in early September.

I signed on and smoked a bowl of Moroccan hash with Albert to seal the deal. Our conversation rambled on until his secretary brought the next meeting to his attention.

Later, Grossman became my manager when I joined The Electric Flag with Mike Bloomfield in 1967. Over the course of his career, his client roster included not only Dylan, but Joan Baez, Odetta, Todd Rundgren, Peter, Paul and Mary, John Lee Hooker, Ian and Sylvia, Phil Ochs, Gordon Lightfoot, Richie Havens, The Band, Jesse Winchester, Janis Joplin, The Electric Flag and The Pozo-Seco Singers.

The next thing Grossman had to do was to put the band together.

Michael Bloomfield wanted to keep his gig with the Paul Butterfield Blues Band so he passed on the Dylan shows, as did drummer Bobby Gregg, who was over-committed with his studio session work.

Mary Martin, Albert's assistant, was originally from Canada and had heard Levon and the Hawks playing on Yonge Street at Friar's Tavern in Toronto. It was Mary who convinced Dylan to go to Canada to hear them.

Dylan was so impressed with Levon Helm, the drummer, and Robbie Robertson, the guitarist, that he hired them. About a week later, I got a call from Dylan's management office to be at the Carroll Music rehearsal studio at 625 West 55th Street to begin preparation for the two concerts.

It was at Carroll's that I met Robertson and Helm for the first time. I was set up with a Fender Bassman amp for rehearsal, which I used on stage for the concerts. We began what would be two weeks of intensive rehearsals for the Forest Hills and The Hollywood Bowl concerts.

The new guys totally changed the feel of the band. Robbie Robertson and Mike Bloomfield are both very energetic guitar players, but totally different in style. Bloomfield was spontaneous with his parts, while Robertson was stiffer and far more precise. Where Bobby Gregg was a solid drummer right in the pocket.

Levon was always on the edge. It's always "Uh oh, are we gonna make it? Yeah!" You always made it. But there was a natural tension with everything Levon did. It's a style that helped to create the sound of The Band later on. Bob related to it.

Because the songs were so strong in their identity, the addition of Robbie and Levon added to what Al and I had originally worked out in the studio. After some rehearsals, we began to relax. But it was tense until we got familiar with each other. Levon and I spent some time hanging out in the village after rehearsal just talking about what was going on in our lives at that time, including the women. I was in the midst of a breakup with my girlfriend Chris who was the line captain of the chorus line at the Latin Quarter nightclub. She would come down to the Sniffen Court Inn where I was playing, after her show, and we would hang out. It seems she had a boyfriend I didn't know about and she chose him. When I asked why not me she said, I always know where he is, with you I don't. Levon, who advised me I was better off without her, was a southern country boy cracking jokes about all the beatnik type hippie chicks, talking about the complications, the opportunities, getting high and Bob's music, which neither of us knew much about.

Levon and I were at The Dugout on Bleeker Street eating some steak tidbits, my favourite Dugout meal and taking it all in. Later, we walked by the Kettle of Fish on MacDougal Street and saw Bob, Al and Bobby Neuwirth, Bob's road manager, hanging out. We opted to continue our conversation and new friendship over a cup of coffee downstairs at the Gaslight Café listening to Phil Ochs, writer of the Joan Baez hit "There but for Fortune," and Jim and Jean who I would later write, record and perform with.

Later that night, I got a call from Paul Harris, my keyboardist friend, to play on an album for the English duo John and Beverley Martyn called *Stormbringer!* I mentioned to Paul that I was hanging out with Dylan's new drummer, Levon Helm, and did he need a drummer. Paul called producer Joe Boyd, then called me back and said bring him down. When I told Levon about the session, he said, "I just play the way I play, no fancy stuff." I responded, "If it's good enough for Dylan, I'm sure it will be good enough for John and Beverley Martyn."

With two weeks of rehearsals behind us, we were ready for Forest Hills. The tennis court was originally built in 1923 as the home of the U.S. Tennis Open. The stadium had hosted the Beatles and

Barbara Streisand the year before. The Rolling Stones, Simon & Garfunkel, Jimi Hendrix, The Who and Frank Sinatra would play there around the time of our concert.

August 28 was a typically hot and humid summer day, but as the evening approached the temperature began to drop. It soon became cold and windy. The stage where we were to perform was set back some distance from the stadium itself, which held about 15,000 fans. Due to the stage lighting, we couldn't see the audience — only the deep green lawn in front of us.

Dylan had gone electric a month earlier at the Newport Folk Festival. His fans were not happy. The uncertainty about what would happen at Forest Hills, his first live performance since Newport, was running high. The audience was self-righteously hostile and they didn't hide it. The show got off to a surreal start when the crowd learned that the master of ceremonies was "Murray the K" Kaufman, a rock impresario and Top 40 disc jockey. This didn't sit well with the folk music audience there to see the "pure" Bob Dylan. Kaufman was greeted with loud boos and jeers from the audience.

Al and I were standing next to Albert Grossman, who was wearing a mischievous Cheshire cat grin on his face to indicate that he was enjoying the spectacle surrounding his artist. It was the first time I witnessed Albert's sarcastic sense of humor and his take on the music business. He knew that however the audience reacted — good or bad — it would boost Bob's notoriety and uniqueness. He was dead-on right.

The show began with Bob doing his acoustic solo set. He opened with "She Belongs to Me" and did "Gates of Eden," "Love Minus Zero/No Limit," "Desolation Row" and "It's All Over Now, Baby Blue." The closing solo was "Mr. Tambourine Man." The opening set seemed to calm the crowd.

For me it was like being a gladiator in the Roman Coliseum,

waiting in the wings while the crowd held its collective thumb in a middle neutral position. The thumb was pointing up after Bob finished his acoustic set, but as the amps and drums begin to make their appearance on the stage, the thumbs started to drop.

During the intermission, Bob cleared the backstage area and called for a band meeting. "I don't know what it will be like out there," he told us. "It's going to be some kind of carnival. Go out there and keep playing no matter how weird it gets!"

Set Song List for the Electric Set

1. Tombstone Blues
2. I Don't Believe You (She Acts Like We Never Have Met)
3. From a Buick 6
4. Just Like Tom Thumb's Blues
5. Maggie's Farm
6. It Ain't Me, Babe
7. Ballad of a Thin Man
8. Like a Rolling Stone

As the band walked onto the stage, the temperature took a steep drop and the wind blew harder. We could hear the ominous grumbling of fans happily sitting in judgment. Though we couldn't see them, we could feel the tension in the cold night air. We kicked off with "Tombstone Blues" to loud jeers and boos, which faded into mixed approval and applause by the end of the song. It was during the fifth song, "Maggie's Farm," that some of the fans jumped out of the seating area and ran across the green grass toward the stage. I only noticed it when I saw numerous security guards tackling folks as they came onto the stage.

Bob never missed a beat and the band played on! I watched Al fall, as his organ stool was pulled out from under him. Levon held his own as the crowd rushed at him. Bob, Robbie and I were towards the front of the stage. Robbie and I moved closer to Bob, who had a strange, maniacal grin on his face. When we got to "Ballad of a Thin Man," Bob played the intro on the piano over and over again until the audience quieted down. I added that move to my "do and don't" list of on-stage tactics. The concert finally closed with "Like a Rolling Stone" — drawing cheers from the same audience that had booed us earlier.

The moment the show ended, Bob disappeared. He had left the stadium in his limo leaving us sidemen to fend for ourselves. Road manager Bobby Neuwirth and his crew would take care of our instruments and other gear. I left with Al, after weaving our way through the crowd, experiencing hot and cold crowd recognition up close for the first time.

After locating my car, we made our way back to Albert Grossman's apartment on Manhattan's lower west side for the after-show party, where we found a smiling Bob Dylan and a very satisfied Albert Grossman. It was here that I first met Grossman's wife, Sally, a sophisticated, warm woman. She is also the elegant lady in red, smoking a cigarette on the cover of the Dylan album, *Bringing It All Back Home.*

New York Times critic Robert Shelton's review of the concert in the New York Times:

August 30, 1965

Folk Singer Offers Works in 'New Mood' at Forest Hills

By ROBERT SHELTON

Facing a rude and immature audience, Bob Dylan gave a program Saturday night at the Forest Hills Music Festival in Queens in which he was a model of patient composure.

40

Some 15,000 persons packed the tennis stadium for a program by the widely imitated and highly controversial young singer-guitarist-songwriter. Most of the audience's attitudes were concerned with Mr. Dylan's excursions into "folk rock," a fusion of rock 'n' roll with folk-based songwriting.

The first eruption came when Jerry White, a radio announcer associated with folk music, introduced Murray (the K) Kaufman, a disk jockey associated with rock 'n' roll. Mr. Kaufman was barely able to shout his blessings on Mr. Dylan and his new mood before the audience howled and booed its disapproval.

After a delay of several minutes, Mr. Dylan appeared alone with his guitar, harmonics, plaintive voice and seven of his folkish songs.

Among them was a major new work, "Desolation Row," a long work filled with the incongruities of black humor and macabre imagery. The song, another of Mr. Dylan's musical Rorschachs capable of widely varied interpretation, ranged freely from Cinderella to T.S. Eliot to "Einstein disguised as Robin Hood." It can best be characterized as a "folk song of the absurd."

After intermission, Mr. Dylan appeared with an excellent rock 'n' roll quartet, with Robbie Robertson playing the electric guitar, Al Kooper the electric piano, Harvey Brooks the electric bass, and Levon Helm the drums.

The electric band and the high-voltage vocalizing raised the level of Mr. Dylan's performance from the intimate introspective vein of the first half to a shouting crackling intensity. The young audience's displeasure was manifested at the end of most of the numbers, by booing and shouts of "we want the old Dylan." The young star plowed valiantly on, with the sort of coolness he has rarely displayed on stage.

He even kept his coolness during repeated sorties of very young members of the audience who ran onto a roped-off grass section in front of the stage, after, or during, songs. Several eluded the guards and got to the stage, but were evicted. Mr. Dylan just kept singing.

Nothing so dramatized the childishness of the audience's reaction to folk rock than when it ceased to boo and started to sing along with the popular song, "Like a Rolling Stone." Evidently the hostility extends only toward things with which they aren't familiar.

By the time they get to know his excellent new folk rock songs, such as "Tombstone Blues," maybe the noisy young boors who ruined an artistically strong concert may have grown up a bit.

We took off for Los Angeles on Sept. 3, 1965 for the concert at the Hollywood Bowl. Robbie, Levon and I were told we were flying across the country on a private plane, while the others flew commercial. We were excited to think we had our own plane. What we weren't told was the flight was aboard Grossman's Lockheed Lodestar, a World War II puddle jumper that would take 12 hours and would make three or four stops for fuel. Basically, we kept the band's equipment company, saving Albert travel expenses.

It was my first flight to Los Angeles and I exhaled when we landed on the tarmac. We took the introductory tour of the LA freeway system, weaving our way toward the Hollywood Sunset Hotel on Sunset Boulevard. Al and I were roommates. We stayed just down the hall from Bob's suite. We had two days until the concert.

A songwriter named P.F. Sloan had called Bob to set up a meeting. Kooper and I were hanging out in Dylan's room when the call came in. Sloan had written "Eve of Destruction," which was a big hit for Barry McGuire. The song was obviously a Dylan imitation. Bob — playing the role of the spider drawing a fly into his web — was prepared for a "slice and dice" meeting with Sloan. I had seen him use the same cutting down-to-size device in tandem with Grossman many times before. Both Bob and Albert enjoyed the edge of their mutual sarcastic banter. Sloan was no match for Dylan. He lasted about 10 minutes before Dylan dismissed him with the word "derivative" burned into his brain.

As we drove up the long driveway to the entrance of the backstage area of the Hollywood Bowl, I could see the Dylan fans entering the venue. I couldn't help but notice how different their attire and attitude was than those at Forest Hills. The California audience was laid back. They got what we were doing right off the bat.

Setlist, Bob Dylan at the Hollywood Bowl

Acoustic

1. She Belongs to Me
2. To Ramona
3. Gates of Eden
4. It's All Over Now, Baby Blue
5. Desolation Row
6. Love Minus Zero/No Limit
7. Mr. Tambourine Man

Electric

1. Tombstone Blues
2. Just Like Tom Thumb's Blues
3. From a Buick 6
4. Maggie's Farm
5. It Ain't Me, Babe
6. Ballad of a Thin Man
7. Like a Rolling Stone

I was standing next to Bob, about to play for a mix of movie stars, folkies and hippies. For me, it was mind-boggling. Keeping my cool, I casually took in the surreal view from the stage. At the Hollywood Bowl, there was a moat that separated the audience from the stage area. But I could make out the faces of the first two or three rows, spotting the likes of Gregory Peck, Mel Brooks, Peter Fonda and Johnny Cash watching from below.

We started off with "Tombstone Blues," the same as Forest Hills. Except, this time there were smiles and dancing people in the audience. The set was loose, but we all followed Bob and made all the endings together.

Bob started blowing on his C harp — I forget which tune it was

— but he couldn't get the instrument to play. He stopped and asked the audience, "Anyone out there got a C harp?" Within seconds, someone in the audience threw a harmonica across the moat that separated the fans from the stage. It landed right at Dylan's feet. He picked it up and began to play. It was sublime intervention if I ever saw it.

The Hollywood Bowl concert was a major success. Al had sped off in the limo with Bob while I was backstage talking to a young lady named Bobbie, who was an actress in L.A. She offered to give me a ride to the hotel, but somehow we took a slight detour and I ended up at the beach in Malibu swimming with her in the moonlight. When I got back to the hotel, the after-concert party had ended.

I had to get to the airport the next day to fly back to New York City to rehearse for a three-week gig in Detroit with vocalist Chico Holiday that I had booked before I met Bob. It was not the best time to leave town for three weeks, but the gig was booked and I was committed. Chico Holiday in later years became a pastor at the Calvary Chapel in Yorba Linda, California.

When I checked in with management from the Cadillac Square Hotel in Detroit as to when the next rehearsals would start, I was told by Grossman's office that they had hired the rest of Levon and Robbie's band, The Hawks, who would be replacing Al and myself on future shows. I was disappointed, but I learned that the other side of acceptance is rejection. Losing jobs like that are a fact of life for professional musicians.

As it turned out The Hawks, who would change their name to The Band, were the perfect fit for Bob Dylan. The rest of the story is rock history. I did not work with Bob again until his *New Morning* album in 1970.

CHAPTER 4

An Act of Prejudice and a Name Change

1965: U.S. President Lyndon B. Johnson signs the Voting Rights Act into law.

My gig with Chico Holiday was in Wyandotte, Michigan, 11 miles outside of Detroit at a small jazz club, The Pier 500. Our opening show went well and the crowd from what I could see from the stage was into the band. When the first set ended, Chico gave each of the band members an official introduction. I was introduced: "And on bass, Harvey Goldstein."

I noticed four guys who were standing directly in front of me by the stage. During the set, they had been smiling and enjoying the music until they heard my name. All of a sudden, the smiles completely left their faces and they walked purposely out of the club. At the time, I noticed it, but didn't think much about it.

At the break, I went out the back door of the club to smoke a cigarette. It was then that I spotted the four men outside — waiting for me. They started calling me "Fat Jew boy," "kike" and other anti-Semitic racist stuff. "Whoa!" Then they started punching me. My first thought was to protect my hands so I could continue playing bass. I began fighting them off with my elbows and kicking them, rather than using my hands. Then I got a lucky break. The back door opened and two men and a woman walked out. The four thugs backed off and left quickly. I was shaken. It was my first experience with blatant anti-Semitism.

At my next gig, I would be surrounded by fellow Jews. After leaving Detroit, I was booked into Grossinger's Hotel in the Borscht Belt of the Catskill Mountains. Opened in 1910, Grossinger's was the home to many famous comedians — such as Don Rickles, Buddy Hackett, Alan King, Joan Rivers and many others. Eddie Fisher and Elizabeth Taylor were married there, and the resort was the inspiration for the 1987 film, *Dirty Dancing*.

Upper-, middle- and working-class Jewish New Yorkers frequented the Borscht Belt hotels with their children and grandchildren, particularly in the 1940s, 50s and 60s when they were denied accommodations in other hotels and vacation resorts because of their Jewishness. Grossinger's was considered one of the most glamorous hotels in the Catskills.

I checked into my room at the staff quarters and then went to eat at a nearby diner. As I was sitting at the table waiting for my order, reflecting on the anti-Semitic incident at the Detroit gig, I happened to glance out the window.

My eyes were drawn to a brilliantly lit billboard that said, "Nat Brooks Orchestra at the Raleigh," another nearby resort hotel. At that moment, I had an epiphany. I would become professionally known as "Harvey Brooks." I would take a showbiz name. It seemed at the time to be the path of least resistance and good business. I wanted to be recognized for my skills and talent rather than dealing with anti-Semitism. It has been fashionable in the entertainment business to have a stage name. So I took one.

When I returned to New York City in 1966, I created a "Doing Business As (DBA)" under the name of Harvey Brooks. The *Highway 61 Revisited* album has the only union session contract and album credit with Harvey Goldstein on bass.

In 2001, while living in Tucson, Arizona, after 9/11, when security tightened at banks and airports, both Bonnie and I had to legally change our names to accommodate the use of our professional name. I became Harvey Goldstein Brooks. I'm proud of my 2,500-year-old Jewish heritage and no name change will ever affect that.

CHAPTER 5

Chemistry and Personality

1965: Early Bird, the first commercial communications satellite, is launched.

While playing on the *Highway 61* sessions with Bob Dylan and some of New York's finest studio musicians, I was able to plug into the workings of a successful chemistry that Dylan had created after much trial and error.

As Bob ran the song down in the studio, the musicians all listened, figuring out the rhythm pattern and chord changes he was playing. From this, we created our own parts to fit into the song. The interaction between what matters — in this case Dylan's song and its properties, the chords, rhythms and melodies — created a new musical genre, folk-rock.

While Dylan was running the first song down, I looked over at drummer Bobby Gregg who, catching my eye, sent me his bass drum pattern via tapping over his heart with the fingers of his right hand. That meant follow my foot (bass drum pattern). I hadn't had any rehearsals nor heard any of the songs. I was also replacing a bassist who hadn't worked out. Bobby's helping hand (or foot) was greatly appreciated.

Setting up a comfortable feeling or groove that supports the basic rhythm pattern of the chord progression is what I was looking to do. After the initial rush of being in the studio at this professional level, I settled down. Once that groove — or pocket — was established, I could add the colorations such as pickups, bridges or fills that help to establish the roadmap of the song. This roadmap starts at the beginning of the song, introducing new sections (or landmarks and bridges), until the end of the tune is reached.

The music is alive as it evolves. In the studio, when the music comes together, that performance becomes *the* take. Once achieved, the recording stands on its own, my work is done.

As a session musician, I've walked into the studio and been handed a chart with nothing but a chord progression on it. All the musicians on the session had the same chord chart. I look around, no vocalist, no leader, just a chord chart engineer and producer.

That producer had a chemistry in mind when he hired each player based on their skill and personality. We were expected to create the songs for our session pay and that's what we did. After we laid down the tracks and left, the producer brought the singer in. They rewrote the melody and lyrics to fit what had just been recorded. They then had the song.

At a session in New York City, I met session drummer Bernard Purdie, who played with Aretha Franklin, King Curtis and The Beatles among many other well-known artists. When I walked into the studio, the first thing I saw was his drum kit in the middle of the studio with two big signs on the wall behind him. The first one said, "Pretty Purdie"; the second, "The Hit Maker." I hadn't met Bernard before, but his personality pervaded the whole session. He truly lived up to his self-promotion and made that session happen.

Just like Purdie, when I walk into a studio I'm expected to make something happen that provides a feeling of confidence and musical foundation to help create a bond between musicians. Miles Davis' *Bitches Brew* album was all about personality and how Miles' acerbic take on life generated direction and inspiration to create a musical chemistry that still resonates.

I had to find my place in the universe called Miles. I went with what I do naturally, respond to the drummers and make spaces for the melody. In this case, it was easy because the drummers were Jack DeJohnette, Don Alias, Lenny White and Billy Cobham.

In concert, the recorded music becomes the starting point of a new chemical reaction. When I played Forest Hills and The Hollywood Bowl with Dylan, the environment had changed. We had a different drummer, Levon Helm, and a different guitar player, Robbie Robertson. The concert was successful because in choosing the new players, the chemistry between the personalities jelled. The playing was different, but the essence or substance of Dylan's music brought all of us together.

When I moved to Woodstock in 1970, I put a band together called The Fabulous Rhinestones. It had personality and chemistry, but something was missing. Maybe it was the name. After all, a rhinestone is a fake gem! The band was managed and signed to Michael Lang's Just Sunshine Label.

We recorded three albums. On our first tour, The Eagles opened up for us. The next year we opened for Stevie Wonder, War and then Sly & the Family Stone. That was the beginning of the end. Being the opening band is never a good position because the audience genuinely doesn't give a shit about you. In the middle of a ballad, "Stevvvie" or "Sly, Sly, Sly" would ring out from the back of the theatre. Sly's already an hour late and the audience by this time hates us.

The band went down the path of Spinal Tap. We'd pull up to a bar in the middle of nowhere with our truck full of equipment and set up our PA and stage amps and play for a couple of hundred people. By the second set the whole place would be full of happy drunks and by the end of the night it would be like the Blues Brothers at Bob's

Country Bunker.

At the same time, a musician's skill or mastery of their instrument has nothing to do with personality or chemistry. It has to with hard work and education. I have been on stage with musicians who only looked at the music, no smiles, no how are you doing, cold as day-old pizza. As soon as the first song was counted off and we started playing, everything just clicked.

Over the years, while on tour, I would take music books with me and when I was back at the hotel I would listen to people like Miles Davis, Horace Silver, John Coltrane, Otis Redding and James Brown. I would study those music books. The thing I had going for me was that when opportunity knocked, I was able to answer the door.

I have been playing the electric bass for more than 50 years. It has been a source of joy, disappointment, frustration and acceptance. My one constant is that the more time and study I put into my playing, the more choices of what I can play or create become available to me.

Early in my career, I got gigs because I was easy to get along with and I genuinely cared about making whatever music I was playing sound good. It was fortunate for me that most of the gigs at that time were with more experienced players that I could learn from. They liked the fact that I would listen to what they said and what they played. I was in a melting pot of cultures and colors of people that accepted me into their fold. It was all about the music.

I have always respected and accepted the artists I have worked and played with. Riding in cars, vans, motor homes and buses allowed me to spend time with people whose opinions and thinking were different than mine.

Later in my career — as the mode of transportation evolved onto buses and airplanes — I remember a 1982 tour I did with Clarence Clemons, Bruce Springsteen's "Big Man," and his band, The Red

Bank Rockers. The band was mixed between young guys and old guys, experienced and local musicians, smokers, non-smokers and poker players.

The minute we got off the plane and onto our tour bus, the games began. Clarence Clemons was a good bandleader. He'd find ways to keep the band laughing, but always professional. We started playing cards and he came up with this game called Follow the Queen. Every time a Queen showed up as an open card in seven-card stud, the next card would be wild. Money moved around the table as winning and losing kept shifting. Funny how a poker game kept the band in touch with each other. And on the bandstand there was a chemistry created by constant riffing, jokes and stories that were shared around the table and then onto the "Big Man" stage at showtime.

What it all comes down to is that the catalysts that connect artists to their audience are chemistry and personality. You either have it or you don't!

CHAPTER 6

Greenwich Village, Late 1965: The Right Place at the Right Time

Oct. 1965 — The U.S. began the bombing of Cambodia despite its neutrality in the Vietnam War.

If you were a musician, folk singer, poet, comedian or visual artist, Greenwich Village was the place to be in the 1960s. I started going to the Village in 1963 to hear jazz at places like the Village Vanguard, Village Gate and The Half Note. I heard Monk, Coltrane, Mingus, Miles and all the greats play there during this amazing time.

The Night Owl Café on MacDougal Street was where John Sebastian's Lovin' Spoonful developed. Gerdes Folk City on Mercer, The Bitter End on Bleecker Street, the Kettle of Fish on MacDougal and Café Wha?, also on MacDougal at the corner of Minetta Lane, were among the coffee houses and bars where cash-hungry musicians would take their chances at open mic nights. Bob Dylan recorded an early version of his classic song, "Masters of War," one night in the basement at Gerdes.

Opened in 1958 as a "basket house" where performers worked for tips in a basket, the dark, steamy, subterranean Gaslight began by showcasing beat poets, including Allen Ginsberg and Gregory Corso. By the 1960s, the Gaslight became known as a folk club after Sam Hood took over management. He brought in performers like Phil Ochs, Dave Van Ronk, Buffy Saint Marie, Jim and Jean and Eric

Andersen to perform. We musicians and folkies didn't think much about making money in those days. We went to the Village to be heard and seen. To perform in the Village in those days was to be a true artist.

The Paris artist colony known as the Left Bank did not last 100 years. Yet Greenwich Village is over 400 years old. The Marlton House on West 8th Street between 5th and 6th Avenue was the home to many writers and poets who found the apartments cheap with neighbors that offered up the Bohemian lifestyle.

That lifestyle helped their creative juices flow. It was here that Jack Kerouac wrote *The Subterraneans*. Also, Valerie Solanas, the infamous stalker of Andy Warhol, lived at the Marlton. She wanted Warhol to produce her play, *Up Your Ass*. After a dispute, she shot him. Her story became urban legend.

The Café Au Go Go at 152 Bleecker Street and Steve Paul's The Scene at 301 West 46th Street both opened in 1964. They served as hangouts for a bohemian niche of actors, musicians and theatre workers. Johnny Winter played at The Scene and Rick Derringer's band, The McCoys, were the house band there. The Velvet Underground and Nico made several appearances in early 1967, while Tiny Tim, strumming his ukulele, became a regular opening act. Headliners included Tim Hardin, The Doors and the Jimi Hendrix Experience, who made their New York debut at The Scene in July 1967.

More than 50 years later, there are new stages with a new generation of performers. Yet I still have vivid memories from that era, undiminished by the passage of time. I can't say if the music was better back then. Only the years will tell us that. But my memories of that time still burn deep and will so for the rest of my life.

Armed with the reputation of working on *Highway 61 Revisited* and a new name, I descended on Greenwich Village ready to make my mark. To say it was the right place at the right time sounds like a cliché, but it was true. I knew I had to be in the Village to get work, but the people I met in such a short time were extraordinary by the standards of any era.

At that time I was still living in Queens Village with my parents, so I traveled regularly in my Mustang each evening to the other village. My gig of choice was at the Cafe au Go Go, a basement coffee house owned by Howard and Ellie Solomon, who cared more about the quality of the music they presented than making money. The place became a hub for many well-known folksingers like Odetta, Judy Collins, as well as Lenny Bruce, the groundbreaking comedian of the times.

My introduction to the club was on Sunday, March 14, 1965. It was "A Tribute to the Memory of Charlie Parker" with Jackie McLean, Lee Konitz, Hank Mobley, Joe Henderson, Freddie Hubbard, Blue Mitchell, Barry Harris, Walter Davis Jr., Benny Powell, Richard Williams, Kenny Burrell and Betty Carter. As I was leaving the club, I introduced myself to Howard Solomon, who was standing by the exit door talking to people as they left.

A few months later, after completing the Dylan sessions, I went to see Howard about the possibility of playing at his club. He suggested that I should hang out and meet people. I took his advice and it paid off — big time. I blended in intuitively and began playing with many of the artists who were performing there.

Eventually, just by being there, I became known as the bass player in residence. My basslines developed a reputation and I played with Richie Havens, Skip James, Fred Neil, Tim Hardin, Jim and Jean and Eric Andersen. In those days, one never really knew what was going to happen or with whom.

Tim Hardin

One night Tim Hardin was performing. He wrote some classic songs including "If I Were a Carpenter," recorded by everyone from Joan Baez, Johnny Cash and Robert Plant to Bobby Darin and The Four Tops. "Reason to Believe" was covered by Rod Stewart, The Carpenters and Glen Campbell, among many others. But Hardin was a heroin addict and a notoriously erratic performer.

Tim was going to do a solo set on guitar and decided at the last minute to add bass, guitar and piano. I was backstage talking to Richie Havens when Solomon asked me to play the set with Hardin. I had never met Tim before and didn't really know what to expect.

About an hour and a half before the show, we rehearsed "If I Were a Carpenter" and "Reason to Believe," among others. The music was tight and Tim seemed comfortable. Just before it was time to go on, the band met backstage to refresh and work out any problems we saw at rehearsal. Tim was nowhere to be found. We waited and waited for him. He finally arrived 20 minutes after the show was set to begin. Tim had gotten high and was totally incoherent. This was my initiation into the junkie and alcoholic disappointment club.

We started the set with "Don't Make Promises You Can't Keep" instrumentally and after a while he stumbled onto the stage, grabbed the mic and started mumbling and drooling. The audience, realizing Tim was blasted, started to yell at him and egg him on. Tim reacted by unzipping his pants fly and pulling out his dick, screaming, "You want a show, here's your fucking show."

We all kept playing, though in a state of amazement as this fiasco played out. Finally, Soloman, the owner, mercifully led Tim off the stage. Later, I played with Tim at the Newport Folk Festival and it was an incredible set. Tim Hardin was one of the best — just totally unpredictable.

Fred Neil

 I was introduced to Fred Neil, writer of "Everybody's Talking" from the movie *Midnight Cowboy* by John Sebastian on stage at the Cafe Au Go Go during his marathon gig from June third to June 19, 1966 with musicians like Al Kooper (organ or guitar), me or Felix Pappalardi on bass, John Sebastian (harp), Dino Valenti (guitar) and Karen Dalton (guitar). Fred and I hit it off and began playing together. Through Fred I met Karen Dalton, who I would later produce for Just Sunshine Records.

My next meeting with Fred was in 1970, when I began to produce Karen's album in Woodstock. Fred had moved up to

Woodstock to start writing and collecting songs for his next album. I loved playing music with Fred. His voice, songs and timing were exceptional, making him the complete performer.

Montreux Jazz Festival

On July 11, 1975 I joined Fred, with John Sebastian on harp and Pete Childs on guitar, making a rare appearance at the Montreux Jazz Festival. Fred was fantastic.

The setlist included:

1. The Dolphins
2. That's the Bag I'm In
3. Little Bit of Rain
4. The Other side of This Life
5. Nashville Cab
6. Stories We Could Tell
7. December's Dream
8. Everybody's Talking
9. Candy Man

Mike Lang, who was now Fred's manager, had us woken up the next morning to drive five hours from Montreux, Switzerland, through many small villages created to serve the king's many palaces, stopping at one to partake in a five-star meal and then on to Paris to do a radio show.

We arrived in Paris on July 14, which unknown to me was the celebration of the French Revolution's Bastille Day. People were dancing on the car roofs as they were winding through streets filled with partying Parisians. We worked our way through the masses and got to the radio station just in time to do our show.

We stayed at The Esmeralda Hotel across the Seine from Notre

Dame Cathedral. As I recall, someone at the hotel told us that Memphis Slim was playing piano at a club nearby, so we immediately rushed out to find him and we did. He was playing in a club that had no decorations on its stone walls, but the sound was great and Slim was awesome.

Rolling Coconut Revue

With Peter Childs, Fred Neil & John Sebastian at Rolling Coconut Revue, Coconut Grove Playhouse. Photo courtesy Catherine Sebastian

Two years later as part of the "Rolling Coconut Revue" Fred and John invited me to join them in playing a concert to raise money and awareness for getting a ten-year moratorium on the whaling industry at the Tokyo Harumi International Trade Center.

We flew from San Francisco to Tokyo. This was my first gig

there and had no idea what to expect. After about 15 hours of drinking and storytelling we arrived in Tokyo. When that cabin door opened it was like stepping into a decompression chamber. We all composed ourselves and headed for the baggage and customs area. It seemed very serious and rigid, but they still managed to lose my baggage which would never be found. There were too many musicians to mention but there was only one Wavy Gravy breaking any uncomfortable moment with understanding and laughter.

The concert was a huge success. The moratorium was achieved and the musicians had a great time helping a worthy cause.

Recording with Fred at Bayshore Studios

Fred and his manager Mike Lang called and asked me to record some tunes at Bayshore Studios (Miami) for Just Sunshine Records. Pete Childs would play guitar with me on bass. They asked me to bring some cover tune possibilities from my album collection. I was under the impression that I would be producing just as I produced Just Sunshine's Karen Dalton's album *In My Own Time*.

I flew down and went to Fred's house and camped out for the time I was there. We listened to a Best of Jerry Lee Lewis country album and Otis Redding, amongst others. Fred had good weed. We smoked and played. He found a Bobby Charles tune called "He's Got All the Money." The punch line was "And He Won't Give Me None." Fred had a lot of stories on that subject. Every story he sang was believable whether you believed the words or not. Most of all for me he hit the low notes as well as the high. The album we did was rejected. I was not the producer. There were too many cooks in the kitchen.

Greenwich Village Days

Susie Campbell, who worked with the musician's manager, Arthur Gorsen, introduced me to Eric Andersen. I'd heard him perform a few times at the club. He invited me on stage to play on a couple of his tunes. After the show, we all went back to Eric's loft on Spring Street. This area of factory lofts has now become the fashionable Soho District. In the 1960s artists, musicians, dancers and ragmen selling their wares all inhabited the neighborhood.

Eric's loft was one flight up some very narrow, creaky wooden steps. We followed Eric, and his girlfriend, guitarist and singer Debbie Green (who had been a fixture on the Cambridge folk scene), up the stairs that led into their loft, the first I had ever seen. It was one giant room with only the bathroom and bedroom having walled privacy. In the middle of the room was a comfortable padded chair facing two six-foot tall speakers in a stereo listening configuration. Behind and to the right of the chair, couches were placed.

Eric asked me if I had ever heard Otis Redding. I hadn't, so he signaled for me to sit and then dropped the needle on *Otis Blue*, followed by The Soul Album. I was mesmerized. Otis Redding was magical, seeming to have the same effect on everyone in the apartment. I looked at the back of the *Otis Blue* album jacket to see who the bass player was and then added Donald "Duck" Dunn to my favorite bass player list along with Scott LaFaro, Paul Chambers, Ron Carter and James Jamerson.

It was at Eric's loft that night that I met Jim and Jean Glover, who had stopped by to visit. Jim was about six-feet, three-inches tall with a mustache. Jean was cute, brown-haired and short. Sometime during that evening, they hired me to play some gigs and eventually record with them. When I started working with Jim and Jean, I began sleeping at their Leroy Street railroad-style apartment while we were rehearsing.

This meant I didn't have to commute back and forth to Queens each day. We rehearsed each tune until there was no searching for parts or losing concentration. I was using a pair of Danelectro basses. One was the Longhorn four and the other a six-string for the road gigs (They were so small I could carry both in a single case!) I used the Fender for recording.

I met Phil Ochs at Jim and Jean's flat. Ochs had written "There but for Fortune" that Joan Baez had recorded. Jim and Phil were old college friends from their days together at Ohio State University. Phil had come by the flat to share new music he was working on for his next album. My first impression of Phil was of a very intense guy who was totally involved in his political songwriter's world.

In passing, he mentioned that he would soon be moving out of his apartment on Thompson and Bleecker Street. He asked if we knew anybody who might be interested. The apartment was just around the corner from the Cafe au Go Go. It was a studio walkup on the third floor and the rent was $225 a month. It was perfect for me and I took it on the spot.

To say the least, the new apartment was funky. It had a small fireplace and a decent view out the window. The kitchen was on the right and since there were no windows in the kitchen, it was very dark. I turned on the light and watched cockroaches scurry through the dirty dishes left behind by Ochs in the sink.

The first thing I did was throw a roach bomb in the kitchen and toss the filthy dishes. Then I left for a few hours to let the bomb do its work. When I came back, the wall was totally covered with generations of dying roaches. They came out of the building's foundation to die! Grandfathers, great grandfathers — everyone in the roach family. If you have ever lived in a city or have seen the film *Joe's Apartment*, you will understand that the war between humans and roaches is an ongoing battle.

As I crossed MacDougal Street walking past Figaro's coffee-house, I noticed a sign that had said "Hep Bagel Café" yesterday had changed to "Hip Bagel" today. The heart of the Village baton had virtually passed overnight from the beatniks to the hippies. About that changing scene, Dave Van Ronk said: "The beatniks hated folk music. The real beats liked cool jazz, bebop and hard drugs...but in the eyes of the media, folk music and beatniks were one and the same. So, a lot of people came to the Village to see the beatniks and they ended up seeing folk music."

I'd buy my food, park the car and hang at the Village clubs and restaurants. The Dugout was a saloon bar with sawdust on the floor and swinging doors. It had a great jukebox and catered to musicians, actors, poets and music business people. The Dugout was next door to the Bitter End, directly across Bleecker Street from the Cafe au Go Go.

I was having some steak tidbits, a Dugout specialty, with Jimi Hendrix who I had met backstage at the Go Go when he was playing with John Hammond Jr. and Richie Havens. Suddenly, the doors swung open and in walks Albert Grossman, followed by Dylan. They ignored us completely and went to a table in the back. Dylan then went over to the jukebox and played "Corina, Corina" by Taj Mahal and the Rising Sons and glanced over at us and gave a slight nod. He then went back to his table.

Jimi, Richie and I were talking about whether Richie should get some false teeth since he was completely toothless. He wanted to know how expensive they were and if that would ruin his vocal sound or not. Jimi was asking me about a place to crash after his gig at the Go Go, when a young Dylan fan started gushing loudly to Bob about how much she liked him. That's when Bob's blades of sarcasm sliced her enthusiasm and sent her off in a state of deflated confusion. We all looked at each other, shook our heads and went back to our conversation.

My first road gig with Jim and Jean was at the Chessmate, a coffee house in Detroit booked by Arthur Gorson. There I met the owner, Morrie Widenbaum, a former Michigan State chess champ who had played speed chess with Bobby Fischer. He challenged me to a $10 chess game, which I accepted. It was a quick $10 loss. I was pretty naïve in those days. I should have known better from the name of the club alone!

Opening for us at the Chessmate was a little-known duo, Chuck and Joni Mitchell, from Canada. Joni, with her sexy long blond hair, was mesmerizing. Her voice combined with her guitar style made her quite unique. We were all about 22 years old and none of us thought about the future or the concept of celebrity. But I sensed Joni had that "thing" that would take her far.

Chuck and Joni opened the show and after we did our first set, we went to the dressing room — which was actually in the kitchen. Asleep and sprawled out on a long freezer in a black leather jacket was Neil Young, and sitting cross-legged on the floor was Bruce Palmer, both old friends of Joni's from Canada. Joni woke up Neil and introduced him to us all.

The guys were driving cross-country to L.A. in Young's old Cadillac hearse to join up with Stephen Stills and Richie Furay to create a new band to be called The Buffalo Springfield. After the club closed, we all went to Chuck and Joni's apartment near the club and talked music, politics, life and dreams. For me, that was a chance meeting of musicians passing in the night on the way to their futures.

Into the early morning, Jean and I, inspired by the evening's events, wrote a tune to be titled "One Sure Thing." It was on Jim and Jean's next album, *Changes*, and was later covered by Fairport Convention.

Getting back to my apartment in New York City, it took me a day to wind down and recover from the tour. Miles Davis and Gil Evans' *Sketches of Spain* album played on my turntable, keeping me company. Sipping a glass of wine and, smoking a joint, I ate a corn beef sandwich on rye with mustard from Katz's Deli before dozing off. Fully recovered by 9 p.m., I was out the door with bass in hand and headed to the Cafe au Go Go to play with Richie Havens.

That night Richie's set went well. Among the songs we played were Jesse Fuller's "San Francisco Bay Blues" and Dylan's "Just Like a Woman." Backstage turned into a real party. I got to spend some time with Muddy Waters, who invited me to sit in his dressing room area and offered me a Chivas Regal and champagne chaser. Muddy expounded on the importance of the strong laid-back backbeat in the blues and how important it was to show respect. Muddy's drummer at the time was Francis Clay, a very solid drummer. But Muddy would every now and then turn around and bring his fist down from over his head on the backbeat just to remind him. B.B. King did the same thing with his drummers, a reminder to stay solid.

Later that night, around three in the morning, Otis Spann, Francis Clay and I jammed. What a pleasure that was — something I will never forget.

———

A week later, my apartment at Thompson and Bleecker Streets was robbed while I was working. The third-floor apartment had bars on the windows. The thieves probably came down from the roof, kicked in the bars and walked the stuff out the front door. I suspect they cased the building and had watched me moving my gear into the place. However they did it, the burglars were a lot hipper than I was.

They stole my Fender Precision and Jazz Basses, an Ampeg Baby Bass, which was the first solid-body electric upright bass, my music equipment accessories, all my records, my stereo system and my television set. In short, they cleaned me out. Luckily, my Dan Armstrong basses were at Jim and Jean's apartment and weren't stolen. Since I was on a gig with Richie Havens at the Go Go that night, I had my Epiphone hollow-body bass with me.

As a result of the theft, I bid a fond farewell to the roaches, packed up my remaining possessions and moved out. I found a new apartment on 21st Street between 9th and 10th Avenues. This was a classic railroad apartment that had a series of rooms that were accessed from a hallway that ran the length of the apartment from the front to the back.

The evening I moved in, I was meeting up with my girlfriend, Jill, at the Kettle of Fish in the Village, a hangout for the folk intelligentsia upstairs from the Gaslight Cafe. Jill and I had been going out for about six months and she was planning to move in with me. Jill was a beautiful woman who was very desirable but not the woman I would settle down with. I was on the road a lot and things were beginning to get tense between us and I felt her drifting away. I couldn't blame her.

After drinks and dinner, we planned to go to the apartment. However, differences between us were beginning to gnaw at me and the pending move for her brought things to a head. As a result, we opted to go our separate ways and said good-bye instead. I introduced her to Tom Rush, one of the artists I was working with, and the next time I saw her she was Tom's new album cover.

My mornings at the 21st Street apartment started at noon with my walk down three flights of stairs through a hallway filled with the essence of coffee and the scent of weed. I went around the corner and sat in my booth at the Empire Dinner. I'd pick up a newspaper, read through Mike Lupica in the sports section and about the war in Vietnam. I saved the crossword puzzle for last.

On one of those routine mornings, the phone rang. It was Rick Danko, my replacement as bass player for Dylan's band. My friend, John Simon, had given him my number and suggested that he call me about borrowing my upright bass. He wanted to use it for The Band's first album, *Music from Big Pink*, that John was producing and recording in Woodstock. I told him he could come and pick it up. About three hours later, Rick Danko, Levon Helm, Robbie Robertson, Garth Hudson and Richard Manuel were in my apartment jamming.

Rick began thumping away on the upright. These guys were funny. They started singing songs I'd never heard before with only our basslines to support them. I broke out some wine and Rick rolled a couple of joints. We had a good time laughing and telling stories. Even though I lost the Dylan gig to Danko, I understood how getting a seasoned cohesive killer band to back up Bob Dylan made sense.

In my opinion, Robbie Robertson raped The Band. He claimed all the money and credit and left his partners financially unprotected. Garth Hudson, who is responsible for the musical creativity and sound of The Band, does not have a share in writer or publishing royalties to my knowledge. Levon, Rick and Richard, I miss you guys.

———

It was the summer of 1966 and I was getting a lot of recording session calls. I worked with old friends, including Verve Folkways artists Jim and Jean, Elektra artist Tom Rush and David Blue, a great songwriter in the Dylan tradition though very much a man of his own words.

For me, at this time, smoking pot, drinking wine along with songwriting and political conversation was part of my routine. On one of those summer days, while hanging out at Matt Umanov's guitar shop, Eric Andersen walked in and picked up a guitar and we did this great version of "That's All Right Momma." We were enjoying the rush that comes when the music just flows.

A couple of weeks later Eric asked me to play on his next album for Vanguard. This turned out to be a unique project because we did the album twice. The first time was mostly acoustic with Debbie Green on second guitar and me on bass. The second version was done with Paul Harris on piano and Herbie Lovelle on drums playing the same tunes in a different sequence. I never fully understood why this was done, but I think the idea was to get a fuller and more exciting sound. Both versions were released, as *'Bout Changes and Things, Take 1 and 2.*

One side note on my friend Paul Harris, a world-class arranger and pianist. Paul and I met in high school and were instant musical conspirators. His parents wanted him to go to medical school and become a doctor. Paul chose to be a musician instead. His musical vocabulary ranged through jazz composer Horace Silver, to Beethoven and finally ended up at the Kinks. When I started getting sessions, I asked if he wanted to take the leap to become a professional musician. He was ready. Paul and I have played on many projects together, including Richie Havens' *Mixed Bag*, The Doors' *The Soft Parade*, John Sebastian's *John B. Sebastian* and many others.

About a week later, while at the Dugout on Bleecker Street, Lenny Stogel, an artist manager came over to the table and introduced himself. After a few minutes of shooting the breeze, he called over a stocky, thick-lipped guy in a leather jacket leaning on a guitar case who had been standing at the bar. Lenny introduced me to the Canadian David Clayton-Thomas (future replacement for Al Kooper in Blood, Sweat & Tears). Clayton-Thomas, an ex-boxer, was in the city under mysterious circumstances. But, in those days, so many people were.

I was hired to arrange some demos for Clayton-Thomas. I worked with him at my flat on W. 21st Street and helped him get "Spinning Wheel," "And When I Die" and a couple of other tunes in shape. Then we went into the studio and recorded some of the songs. I left soon after for San Francisco to join the new Mike Bloomfield band.

While I was away, I sublet my apartment to Clayton-Thomas. I left all my possessions in the apartment, including glassware and dishes from my mother, my guitarrón mexicano, my furniture — everything. I expected it would all be there when I returned. When I flew back to play the Bitter End in the Village, I went to check up on the apartment and discovered there was a new lock on the door and a different tenant inside.

Clayton-Thomas would never give me a straight answer about what had happened.

Finally, many years later, at The Electric Flag Woodstock reunion gig (which is absurd in itself considering that The Electric Flag did not play Woodstock), Clayton-Thomas dazzled me with a truly amazing story.

He said that Bennett Glotzer, who was Al Kooper's manager at the time, and Al Kooper called the U.S. Immigration Dept. and had him deported back to Canada and that Kooper was trying to get the band (Blood, Sweat & Tears) back. He told me this far-fetched tale with a completely straight face. Once again, I had learned the hard way that no good deed goes unpunished.

CHAPTER 7

Blowouts at the RKO Theatre

1966: The first Star Trek episode, "The Man Trap," is broadcast. The plot concerns a creature that sucks salt from human bodies.

While playing at the Cafe au Go Go, I had been introduced to Arthur Gorson, who managed most of the artists I was playing with and also had his hand in many other music projects. Gorson also managed Murray Kaufman (known as "Murray the K"), the New York disc jockey who was producing a major three-day series of concerts at the RKO Theatre on 58th Street in New York City to be called "Murray the K Presents Music in the 5th Dimension." The shows would introduce Cream and The Who in their first U.S. appearances. Arthur was helping Murray with production details.

While hanging with Gorson at his office, he showed me a photo of the amplifier set-up specified in the rider for Cream and The Who, both British bands new in the states. He asked if I could help him put this package of gear together. I was in.

What I saw in the picture was a wall of amplifiers behind the bass player and a separate wall of amps behind the guitar player. At that time, sound gear in the United States was still pretty primitive and instrument amplifiers were all the same to me — either Ampeg or Fender. I had never heard of Marshall or Vox amplifiers, except as used by the Beatles when they came here and brought their own gear.

The shows took place in 1967, beginning Saturday, March 25 through Sunday, April 2. There were five shows a day starting at 10 a.m. and lasting until after midnight. Mitch Ryder, without his Detroit Wheels, headlined the event. At the insistence of his producer, Bob Crewe, Mitch was embarking on a solo career and was billed as the Mitch Ryder Show, backed by a 10-piece backup band.

Wilson Pickett and Smokey Robinson were booked to play as well. Smokey, though advertised, never appeared. Still wearing his trench coat, he argued on stage with Murray the K and at one point stormed off the stage and up the aisle to the exit. He did not return. Supposedly, he walked out on the show because Mitch Ryder was billed above him. Others on the bill included The Blues Project (with my old friend Al Kooper), Phil Ochs, Simon and Garfunkel and The Young Rascals.

Murray the K had arranged for Baldwin to supply the amplifiers for the show. At the time, Baldwin was new to building amplifiers and produced only solid-state models at the company's Fayetteville, Arkansas organ plant. Their top-of-the-line "Exterminator" model was built in response to the Vox Super Beatle, then manufactured in England.

So we set up a wall of Baldwin amps. During their first rehearsal, Cream immediately blew them all out. Baldwin had simply not designed their amplifiers with Cream in mind. It was on the problem of these amps that I first met Eric Clapton, Cream's guitarist. I shared a cab with Eric to Manny's Music on 47th Street in order to replace the Baldwins with something more suitable.

Eric was in awe of New York City as he looked out through the window of our cab, while asking me what it was like to play with Mike Bloomfield and Dylan. I told him recording with Dylan was where I met Bloomfield and how playing live in front of a bunch of hostile folkies was a unique experience for me.

It was then that our cab delivered us to Henry Goldrich, the owner of Manny's Music and a good friend of mine who I had met through Al Kooper. Henry had been selling me gear for years.

I introduced Henry to Eric Clapton and explained that Cream was playing their first American concert at the RKO with Murray the K in a few days and we had an amplifier crisis. Cream used a wall of Marshall amps that were not available in the states. Baldwin was sponsoring the show, but their amplifiers could not handle the intense Cream energy. Could he help us? Henry thought it over for a minute and said "no problem."

Clapton and I looked at each other — hoping Henry's solution would work. Henry sent a crew that delivered a wall of Ampeg amplifiers to the RKO theatre. At the next rehearsal, Cream blew up the Ampeg amps as well. Henry's gear soon joined the Baldwins in the basement of the theatre.

After striking out once again, we learned that Cream's gear was actually in America, but at the site of their next gig on the tour. We went into action and the road manager had their Marshall amps and other gear flown to New York for the show. The rest is history.

The Who used Vox Super Beatle amps. They literally destroyed their gear in each performance. The Who had a technician running a virtual factory repairing instruments backstage. He used drills, screws, clamps and glue to piece everything back together in time for the next show. At the end of the run, the band decided it wasn't worth the expense of shipping the abused gear back to England. On their final performance, they boosted the smoke pots into explosive bombs and almost literally blew up their amplifiers. A stagehand with a fire extinguisher had to be summoned to put out the fires. Roger Daltrey broke a total of 18 microphones during the entire run of the show at the RKO.

Right before I started working on the Murray the K show, Mike Bloomfield called to ask if I would be interested in joining a Bloomfield-led band that he and Barry Goldberg were putting together. It would be managed by Albert Grossman. I said "yes," and took the bass seat.

While sitting in the back of the empty RKO Theatre watching a rehearsal of Wilson Pickett's band, I couldn't take my eyes off his fatback pocket drummer, Buddy Miles. Pickett kept shouting, "Drummer! Fifty bucks!"

Known for running a tight ship, Pickett was fining Buddy for every miscue and every little mistake. As I watched, I was amazed by Buddy's unique drumming, but I could see he wasn't happy. I sensed he might be ready to leave Pickett, who had a reputation as a very difficult man to work with.

After the sound check, I introduced myself to Buddy and started telling him about our new band. I asked if he would be interested in talking to the leaders of the band about being our drummer. Buddy, from Omaha, Nebraska, was a free spirit and was definitely open to an escape from life with Wilson Pickett.

I told Michael and Barry about Buddy. (I didn't know yet that they'd already talked to Billy Mundi about being the drummer.) I invited Michael and Barry to come down and check out Buddy at one of the shows. They were impressed.

Billy Mundi was suddenly out. He would keep his gig with Frank Zappa's Mothers of Invention. Buddy had only one requirement: it would have to be Bloomfield, Goldberg and myself — not him — who would tell Pickett that he was leaving the band.

Pickett was recording at Mira Sound Recording Studios at 145 West 47th Street. Buddy had warned us that Pickett was pretty tough to talk with and would not appreciate his leaving. Barry and I waited in the lobby of Mira Sound while Bloomfield went into the studio.

About 15 minutes later, Bloomfield comes running out of the studio with Pickett chasing him — and waving a pistol. "You want Buddy Miles? He's my drummer, not your drummer! I'll say when he goes and when he doesn't go!" Pickett shouted, following us running through the lobby of the hotel as we headed for Buddy's room.

What saved us was Pickett's bodyguards, who grabbed him and held him back. They wouldn't let him follow us up the stairs. We made it to Buddy's room and closed the deal. In our minds, we'd notified Pickett and that was it. We never heard from Wilson Pickett again. Two weeks later, I flew out to San Francisco. Buddy Miles met me at the airport. It was the beginning of my days with The Electric Flag.

CHAPTER 8

Heading West to Start a New Band

1967: Racial violence in Detroit; 7,000 National Guards-men aid police after a night of rioting. Similar outbreaks occur in New York City's Spanish Harlem, Rochester, New York, Birmingham, Alabama and New Britain, Connecticut.

My flight from New York City to San Francisco for Mike Bloomfield's The Electric Flag was in April 1967. Our handpicked drummer, Buddy Miles, picked me up at the San Francisco airport. I tossed my suitcase and gear into Bloomfield's beat up Ford Econoline van with no passenger seats.

While sitting in the front, on the floor, Buddy was motor mouthing me about all the weird and crazy things he'd seen and experienced in the two weeks he'd been in San Francisco. We were heading to Michael Bloomfield's house in Mill Valley, California, where all the rest of the band members were staying. When I talked to Eric Clapton, by the way, I had told him I was going out to San Francisco to play in Bloomfield's new, as-of-yet unnamed band, and he was amazed that Bloomfield would even think of leaving the Butterfield Blues Band, which he much admired.

We crossed the Golden Gate Bridge, driving north up Highway 101 past Sausalito, a small resort town on the bay. We passed rows of single-family houses, kids riding their bicycles in the street, trees and grassy lawns. No buildings were over three stories high. It all reminded me of Malvina Reynolds' tune, "Little Boxes." No question about it — I had left New York City far behind.

Bloomfield and his wife, Susan, lived off the main road with their dog, Harry, in a ranch house with a winding uphill driveway in front. As we drove up, I saw five women sitting cross-legged on the front lawn. Three on one side of the driveway and two on the other. As we pulled up, the ladies stood up to greet us. Buddy introduced them to me as The Ace of Cups, San Francisco's one and only all-female psychedelic rock band.

The Ace of Cups was made up of Mary Gannon (bass), Marla Hunt (organ, piano), Denise Kaufman (guitar, harmonica), Mary Ellen Simpson (lead guitar) and Diane Vitalich (drums). In 2018, they'd regroup and make their long-awaited first album. As I got out of the van, they introduced themselves and invited us to hear them play at the Matrix that evening. They were there to welcome each of us to town, since it was big news in Mill Valley that Michael Bloomfield was creating a new band.

While waiting for Michael, Buddy told me he was thankful to get away from Wilson Pickett. While he loved Pickett's music, Pickett was difficult and not at all easy to work with. Buddy said he was grateful to be out from under the man's thumb.

About an hour later, Bloomfield — "Bloomers" as we called him — showed up. Always enthusiastic, he told us how great the band would be and how we would change the course of musical history. For me — I was trying to take it all in as I pushed myself past the jet lag from my flight. I was in a semi state of shock and thankful for Michael's wife, Susan, who made the transition much easier. Susan was hospitable to all the band members.

She made me feel welcome and comfortable, which helped ease me into this new musical living situation. I roomed with Buddy. It was a tight fit, since I brought one bass and a suitcase and Buddy brought five or six bags, plus his drum kit. We were both big guys! Over the next few days, band members gradually filled up Michael's house. Barry Goldberg, who would play organ, Peter Strazza, the sax player, and Marcus Doubleday, who played trumpet, all arrived. Singer Nick Gravenites was already living in Mill Valley.

I remember sitting in a room with Electric Flag trumpet player Marcus Doubleday and other band members at the Flag's band house (Michael and Susan Bloomfield's home) in Mill Valley. I was listening to Marcus telling me how I should try heroin. It would relax me. This was about a month after I flew in from New York to join the band.

"It takes away all the pain and clears your head so you can focus," Doubleday said. As he's telling me this he's shooting up and explains the process at the same time. When he's done he leans back against the wall, smiles and immediately nods out. For me it was the devil at the crossroads and I was convinced that I had to stay on the side of the angels. What I came to learn is you can never trust a junkie and there I was holding down the bottom, in a band filled with them.

In the original band, Nick Gravenites, Buddy Miles and I were the only non-junkies. For the addicts, getting dope was more important than the gig. The first thing they did when we pulled into town was make the connection to score. If they couldn't score smack they would find whatever they could to get them high. I was a naïve kid from Queens thinking I was being friendly and gave many $5 loans before I figured out I was never going to get any of the money back. I was a mark, a sucker.

Buddy, though he didn't become a heroin addict, went from being a great boogaloo R&B drummer/vocalist from Omaha, Nebraska to (under the influence of psychedelics) a self-centered narcissist. The only time he would listen to anyone else was when he had food stuffed in his mouth. This was the band I was in.

78

When we got the opportunity to go down to Los Angeles to do the sound track for the movie *The Trip,* we packed up our newly acquired instruments from Fender and took off to Los Angeles, headed for Hollywood and our first gig, which I elaborate on elsewhere in the book. Don't you know, that pieces of equipment were mysteriously *being stolen*? Thieves were breaking into our van and selectively stealing one instrument at a time, only a junkie would try to sell that story. Every trip to the studio or restaurants had the potential of us getting pulled over and rousted by the cops because we were always holding, were unabashedly noticeable in our attire and were a racially mixed group.

It seemed that after Michael brought in this guy Minsky from Chicago things went from bad to worse. His main purpose was to provide drugs for those under the influence while pretending to be a road manager.

I remember one night that Nick was over to my house and we were smoking some reefer, playing chess and listening to Muddy Waters on the phonograph when the telephone rang. Feeling pretty mellow I debated picking up the phone, but I did. It was a frantic phone call from Barry Goldberg freaking out saying that the cops had just been over and taken Minsky away. Barry was the first band member to leave the band to clean up.

The Electric Flag Rehearsing at the Heliport

At first, we rehearsed at Michael's house. But after a few sessions, Michael shifted rehearsals to a rented space at a heliport halfway between Mill Valley and Sausalito. It was a working heliport, with take offs and landings during the daylight hours. We rehearsed in an office building adjacent to the helipad. Outside of one office being used by the heliport, the rest was rented out to various bands for rehearsal space. At the time, the tenants were The Electric Flag, Santana, The Quicksilver Messenger Service, Sons of Champlain and The Ace of Cups.

With Mike Bloomfield and Nick Gravenites at the Sausalito Heliport.
Photo by Steve Keyser.

We all hung out checking out each other's rehearsals and arguing over who got the best practice times. Santana was a real Bloomfield fan and listened to our rehearsals and would steal the occasional lick. Quicksilver Messenger Service's John Cippolina was another great guitar stylist I jammed with. There was a definite pecking order at the Heliport. The Electric Flag was the new kid in town, so we ended up with the last and smallest rehearsal space at Heliport and were thankful to get it.

We used the music of Otis Redding, James Brown, B.B. King, Freddy King, Albert King, John Coltrane and Horace Silver to build a common musical vocabulary. All of The Electric Flag's original music came out of those influences. We practiced, created and jammed to develop our sound. We did a few live gigs at small area clubs and schools to give the band some seasoning. It was a discovery at one of these early gigs that led to us finding a name for the band. Initially, we were going to use the name Michael Bloomfield's American Music Band or just, An American Music Band.

One gig we played was at an American Legion Hall north of Mill Valley in Larkspur, California. We were setting up backstage when one of our roadies found an American flag on a two-foot high flag-pole with holes drilled in it. The flag was attached to an electrically motorized base that blew air through the holes. He put the contraption on top of the B3 organ's Leslie, the speaker cabinet.

When he plugged it in, the flag began waving. Somebody called it "an electric flag." That phrase kind of floated around for a while. At a band meeting at Bloomfield's house, we adopted it and officially the group became The Electric Flag. The flag became our mascot and a part of our performing gear.

THE TRIP – April / May 1967

The Trip was a counterculture-era psy-chedelic film directed by Roger Cor-man. It was shot in California on loca-tions that included the Laurel Canyon and Hollywood Hills areas of Los An-geles and near Big Sur. The sound-track, by The Electric Flag, was made up of improvisational jazz, blues and rock themes.

In the film, actor Peter Fonda plays a young commercial director, Paul Graves, who takes his first dose of LSD while going through the

heartbreak of a divorce from his adulterous wife, played by Susan Strasberg. At first, Paul's trip is guided by John, played by Bruce Dern, who has convinced him that an LSD trip is exactly what he needs to get him out of his rut. However, Paul soon runs away and abandons John out of paranoid fear.

The film was edited by Roger Corman to simulate the edgy, racing mind of a person on LSD. To understand the effect, Corman took LSD himself. Other photographic effects included body paint on nude actresses and special lighting during the sex scenes in and out of the clubs, which imitated LSD-induced hallucinations.

The Electric Flag created the music but the early visuals of a band playing in the movie were by Gram Parsons and the International Submarine Band, one of the earliest country rock bands. It had been Fonda's original intention to use the International Submarine Bands' music on the soundtrack, but their contribution was deemed insufficiently psychedelic, or "trippy," for the film.

The Trip was released in late August 1967 at the pinnacle of the Summer of Love. It had a huge cultural impact and grossed six million dollars — a massive sum for a movie that cost only $100,000 to make. It was censored throughout the world and home video release on DVD was delayed until 2004 due to cinema classification problems.

My Personal Back Story on Making Music for *The Trip*

I woke up one morning in March 1967 to the sound of voices and the smell of reefer. Bloomfield was sitting at the kitchen table with a guy who looked like the actor, Henry Fonda, smoking a joint. It was Fonda's son, Peter. They were talking about the band doing the soundtrack for a psychedelic movie, *The Trip*. It sounded like a great idea to me.

A few days later, Albert Grossman, our manager, came to Mill Valley to lay out his basic ground rules for our behavior on the set. We were to be available for promotional opportunities, have a good time, be good boys and play our asses off! We arrived in Los Angeles several weeks later.

One day a UPS truck pulled into Bloomfield's driveway. It delivered a truckload of Fender instruments, including basses, guitars, keyboards and amplifiers. Grossman had gotten the instruments using his Dylan clout. It was a musician's wet dream.

Peter Fonda welcomed us with a truly wild Hollywood party at his home.

The party included Fonda, Jack Nicholson, Susan Strasberg and Dennis Hopper out on the tennis courts with road manager Ronnie Lyons and myself — racquets in hand — playing a match. Inside the house, the Chicago guys Mike Bloomfield, Barry Goldberg and Nick Gravenites were partying in the kitchen with known celebrities, models and Hollywood wannabes. Each had a colorful story. Buddy Miles held court with a plate in hand over at the food table.

As the event wound down, Dennis Hopper offered me a ride back to my hotel, with an added tour of the Hollywood nightlife on Sunset Strip. The streets were alive with roving groups of costumed hippies, with camera shooting tourists, sports cars and limousines.

Hopper pulled into the parking lot behind the Whiskey A Go Go, a nightclub in West Hollywood. It was the first Los Angeles discotheque, and was one of the birthplaces of go-go dancing. There was not enough room on the floor for a DJ booth, so they had a glass-walled booth mounted high above the floor. Joanna Labean, one of the dancers at the Whiskey, designed the official go-go girl costume which consisted of a fringed dress and white boots. Most nights, Johnny Rivers opened the club with his live band. When he was not performing, a female DJ — Rhonda Lane — played records.

We walked into the club as the sounds of Little Anthony and the Imperials on stage singing "Tears on My Pillow" ended. Then the band went right into "Shimmy, Shimmy, Ko-Ko-Bop." I looked up and there were mini-skirted girls dancing above the crowd in a cage. My Hollywood initiation was complete.

I didn't know it at the time, but The Doors, who would become the house band at the Whiskey A Go Go for a short time, would play a major role in my future. The debut of the Oedipal section of "The End" got them fired.

I remember waking up the following morning at my hotel to a scene out of a Robin Hood meets the Renaissance fair. All around the room were the Fonda partygoers dressed in their finest Robin Hood, Sherwood Forest garb. Barry Goldberg explained to me that their presence in our room was because later in the night, after I fell asleep, he had moved his guests into our room where everybody had passed out. These folks were the local hippies who were the extras in the film. What I was also beginning to realize was that they were NOT in costume.

Roger Corman moved us out of the hotel into a rented house that looked like a Mediterranean castle. The interior resembled a Hollywood horror movie set. There were arched walkways, a vaulted ceiling in the living room with a giant fireplace and lots of Mediterranean tile in all the bathrooms. Across the road was another castle-like house owned by Bela Lugosi. It appeared to have only slatted windows and gave off strange emanations.

All-in-all, it was an appropriate setting to inspire the music for *The Trip*. Robin Hood and his merry men and women kept appearing at the castle. Adding to the mix of drug dealers, beach movie bikini-clad actresses, Nico (from the Velvet Underground), musicians and posers all made their way to the castle to check out our band.

On to Monterey Pop...

In 1967, The Monterey Pop Festival was the first documented international rock festival. The producers were Lou Adler and John Phillips, with Alan Pariser and Derek Taylor. Alan Pariser always had the best weed. It combined bands with the more commercial Los Angeles attitude with those having a San Francisco non-commercial vibe. The billing included Jimi Hendrix, Janis Joplin, The Jefferson Airplane, The Grateful Dead, The Mamas and the Papas, The Who, Otis Redding, Hugh Masekela, Ravi Shankar, The Electric Flag and Eric Burdon and the Animals. As many as 50,000 music lovers gathered to watch The Who destroy their instruments and Jimi Hendrix burn his guitar before the Woodstock Festival in 1969.

I drove to the Monterey Fairgrounds from Mill Valley early on Saturday, June 17, 1967 after taking some Owsley acid in a cup of coffee. When I arrived, I started walking the grounds, checking out the food, crafts, headshops and most of all, the people. Strolling the grounds, I saw familiar faces of musicians I knew and didn't know, hippies, movie stars, Hells Angels and old and young concertgoers high on acid and pot. Everyone was enjoying the feeling of peace and love that was filling the air.

After my tour around the grounds, I headed backstage and ducked into a tent in the middle of a conversation between Brian Jones, Michael Bloomfield, and Janis Joplin. The talk centered around how having musicians play these kinds of festivals all over the world would result in a more peaceful planet.

Brian was starting to talk about world peace and his words were sounding like they were in slow motion. At that moment, I noticed the Owsley acid was kicking in. I had a slight tingling sensation and everything around me was in vivid color. The combined vibrations of the previously mentioned musicians were so intense, I had to move on. About that time, the crowd started arriving through the main entrance.

Before the Electric Flag went on to perform, Al Kooper, who was stage manager for the show, invited me and the guitarist Elvin Bishop, from Butterfield's band, to jam in a short set. The band consisted of Billy Davenport on drums, Elvin Bishop on guitar, me on bass and Al Kooper, vocals and organ.

After the set, I went backstage to sync up with the Flag, leaving my bass on stage for the roadies to remove. When I asked our roadie to bring my bass backstage, he went to get it, which was supposed to be on its stand. But it was gone — nowhere to be found. Someone had pilfered my bass right off the stage in front of everyone. Fortunately, I had back-up basses. We were to go on shortly after the Kooper set and I had no time to worry about my missing instrument.

Most of the band members were warming up their hands, lips and instruments. I was having a conversation with Buddy Miles, who was telling me how important it was to kick ass. Bloomfield came over and hugged us, saying what a pleasure it is playing in this great band and how groovy everything was. The smell of reefer had replaced all other odors in the air and we were all feeling nervous and mellow at the same time. The next thing I knew, I was standing on the stage looking out at the audience filled with hippies, tourists and Hells Angels. I'm thinking, "This is amazzzzing."

Michael cued Buddy, Buddy counted off "Groovin is Easy," the horns played the intro theme and then the band kicked in. I looked over at Nick Gravenites, whose head was bobbing as he lifted the mic to sing. He glanced over at Mike and me with a big smile on his face. *"Groovin' is easy, if you know how..."*

We were a tight band; we knew what we were doing and played it as we rehearsed. It worked. The audience went nuts. Though we did very well, we were not a seasoned band. Bloomfield came on stage with a huge reputation, but Buddy Miles was our secret weapon. He really won over the crowd. The band was tight and powerful. We made a big impression. All racial cynics had a field day criticizing our obvious black musician influences, but the audience loved us.

Al Kooper, Buddy Miles, me and interviewer Pete Welding at the Monterey Pop Festival. Photo by Pat Murphy.

That evening, after our set, I was hanging out with Keith Moon waiting for Otis Redding to perform. Keith was the drummer with The Who, a very talented and funny person whom I first met back in March at the "Murray the K" show at the RKO Theatre in New York City. That had been the first American concert for The Who. He told me that automobiles would motor on air cushions and be powered by the sun in the very near future. It was an interesting comment from a maniacal monster drummer who happened to collect cars.

The show they did in New York was restrained compared to what I saw at Monterey Pop. The gear and microphones went flying.

It was a total demolition derby.

Otis Redding, who closed the Saturday line-up, literally got there just in time for the show, exploded onto the stage and mesmerized us. I got to shake his hand and say hello, but it was in passing. I did, however, talk to Duck Dunn, Otis' bass player and a member of Booker T. & the MG's. We traded compliments and stories.

Duck was really my role model for The Electric Flag. He played solid, simple basslines that created nice spaces for a vocalist to sing in. Nice man, great bass player!

On Sunday, I knew Jimi Hendrix would be sound checking in the afternoon. Jimi was an old friend from my Greenwich Village days and was looking to express himself in a significant way on an American stage. I knew he wanted this show to make an impact. He saw me backstage after his sound check and walked over.

We started talking about Greenwich Village, the clubs and Dylan's "Positively 4th Street" and what a cool song it was. We also talked about the night I brought Verve Folkways President Jerry Schoenbaum down to the Café Au Go Go to hear Jimi James and the Blue Flames backing up John Hammond and Ellen McIlwaine.

Hendrix turned down the deal I got for him with Verve Folkways, a division of MGM, because he signed with Eric Burdon and the Animals' bass player Chas Chandler and Michael Jefferies earlier in the week and how more the English pop music world appreciated what he was doing. In New York City then, he was just another local guitar player.

Jimi would finally launch his career as a superstar that Sunday night at Monterey. I was sitting on the stage about 10 feet away, stage right, from Jimi's set up. The last time I heard Jimi play was at the Café Au Go Go in New York with his band. I was expecting the same kind of R&B show, the guitar behind the neck and flashy footwork, but no! In the trio format with Mitch Mitchell kicking ass and Noel

Redding playing his very reserved style, Jimi dominated.

After the festival, Jimi came to my home in Mill Valley. After a few hours of smoking, drinking and listening to James Brown, B.B. and Albert King, Jimi, Michael, Buddy and I went over to the heliport to jam. It was mighty! To my knowledge, that was the only time that Michael and Jimi ever played together, and the first time Jimi and Buddy jammed.

The First Electric Flag Album

Chronologically, *The Trip* soundtrack album was the Flag's first album. *A Long Time Comin'* was the second "first" album. We recorded it at United Western Recorders in Hollywood pretty much live. One of the cover tunes was Howling Wolf's "Killing Floor." We did a burning version that was *the* take. As we hit the last chord, the tape ran out. Anyone familiar with that tune on our album knows that was the take we used. Many people tried to figure out the "effect" at the end of the song. It was simply the tape slowing down as it wound off the reel. In my mind, it sounded perfect.

Most of the tunes on the album were inspired by Stax, Chicago blues or Motown except for Nick Gravenites' "Another Country," which was a Michael Bloomfield arrangement. We were still experiencing Monterey Pop Festival hangover while searching for a place to go after the verse and chorus of the tune. Michael came up with "create an outer space wall of sound". We hooked up every amp in the studio in line, cranked every amp to eleven and let our instruments feedback. What can I say? It was awesome!

Michael and producer John Court took the tapes to New York City for overdubbing. In New York they added percussion, strings, Richie Havens on sitar and Bobby Notkoff on violin and filled the "Outer Space" in the Phil Spector-like "Wall of Sound."

The song, "Another Country," was also used to bust the band for being un-American. We were playing at the Golden Bear in Huntington Beach, California. After the gig, we came back to the motel and Barry, Nick, Michael and myself were listening to the reel-to-reel tape of the gig when there's a knock at the door.

Outside were two Huntington Beach cops. They said, "We have a noise complaint and we want to enter your room." Michael said, "You need a search warrant to come in sir." The officer showed his gun and said, "Here's my search warrant."

They came in and found some reefer and continued into the bedroom where they found some heroin in a saxophone. They cuffed us, took us down to the police station, fingerprinted us and threw us in a holding cell. We called Albert Grossman, who called his Los Angeles lawyer, Bob Gordon, who immediately bailed us out.

I'll never forget sitting in the Orange County courtroom waiting my turn to face the judge and watching young people get jail time for one joint or a gram of hash. This arrest gave us a headline and story in the first issue of *Rolling Stone*.

We had a few meetings in the judge's chambers, who told me how un-American I was because we had the song "Another Country" on our draft dodging, corrupting hippy album. It had the line *"Get yourself another country"* in it, which upset the judge.

Our lawyer got the case dismissed after some backroom dealing. That was my first and last bout with the U.S. justice system.

Richie Havens: Mixed Bag

Richie Havens and myself at the opening of Bonnie's Rock 'n Roll Art & Artifact exhibition at the Museum of Art, Science and Industry/Discovery Museum in Bridgeport, Connecticut. Photo by Bonnie Brooks.

The Electric Flag was going to New York to promote the new album by performing at the Bitter End, Fillmore East, Cheetah and other such venues. John Court, Albert Grossman's partner in Grosscourt Productions, told me they had signed Richie Havens to a management agreement and a record deal with Verve Folkways. He wanted to know whether I'd like to play bass on the album with Richie. And since I was familiar with Richie's music, perhaps I could arrange and write lead sheets for the rhythm tracks. Richie's style is free and unpredictable, and John didn't want to waste time in the studio.

I first met Richie at the Café Au Go Go right after I did the Dylan sessions in 1965.

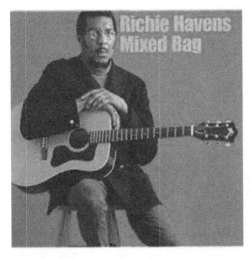

I would come into the club an hour before show time and check in with owners Howard and Elly Solomon as to who would be performing that night. On this particular evening Howard said they were expecting Richie Havens and The Fugs. The Fugs were a legendary New York satirical and self-satirizing rock band led by famous beat poets Ed Sanders and Tuli Kupferberg.

Richie was backstage tuning up his guitar. Howard brought me over to him and told him I was Dylan's bass player. Richie asked me to come up for a couple of tunes and started playing Jesse Fuller's "San Francisco Bay Blues" followed by Dylan's "Just Like a Woman." An hour or so later I was on stage performing with Richie Havens which led to many more nights and eventually Richie's *Mixed Bag* album.

Richie was living in the East Village at this time with his wife and baby. He invited me to come by and I walked over to his apartment. We had played together and Richie and I became friends. As we smoked a bowl of ganja and talked about the songs and how we'd go about putting it all together, our senses were suddenly overcome by a most pleasing scent of Jamaican patties filled with ground beef and mixed vegetables that his wife had cooked up. A bottle of wine came later and after enjoying a delicious meal and playing "Peek a Boo" with the Havens' new baby, we got down to the music.

We got up from the table and went out into the narrow hallway to rehearse. The hallway had a 12-foot ceiling and lots of flat wall space for the sound to echo around us. We started playing "San Francisco Bay Blues," and it sounded amazing in that hallway space. Richie singing the words "Got the blues for my baby down around the Frisco Bay" were magnificent. We played it until it felt good and comfortable. As soon as we hit that sweet spot with the intro and ending, I wrote a rhythm chart and we moved on to other tunes.

Mixed Bag was well received and was one of Richie's most successful. Richie, Bonnie and I remained long-distance friends throughout his lifetime.

The Electric Flag on Tour: Detroit

We pulled off the highway and headed downtown on Woodward Street to our destination, the Strathmore Hotel. It was early evening and I went right up to my room. Bloomfield and the horn section headed out into the night to make whatever drug connections they needed.

My single room had a double bed and a window facing a wall. I turned on the room's one lamp, watched some TV and then fell asleep. About 5 a.m., there was loud pounding on my door. It was the road manager, Gary McPike, saying get packed, we're leaving in 20 minutes.

I staggered down the stairs half asleep, got into one of our vehicles and waited while he rounded up the rest of the band. We drove to the outskirts of town to the Thunderbird Motel. Even funkier! Now, I was rooming with the road manager and he told me that when the junkies went to score that night they got involved with the local black mafia.

We had a mixed band, but one of the white guys got nervous and insulted one of the dealers. That's why we had to get out of town. OK, fine. As a non-junkie, this is one piece of educational information I could have done without. But what's done is done, right? Wrong! That night we went to play the gig, which had become the least memorable part of the story. Then we came back to the motel.

We had a great time playing and the crowd loved it. We were all feeling good. We hung out for a while listening to tapes of the sets that night and then went to bed. Buddy and Mike had the only single rooms. At about 4:30 a.m., there was a knock on the door of our hotel room. Gary, the road manager, opened the door and saw Flag tenor saxophonist Peter Strazza in front of a guy with a gun. And I was awakened with the words, "Roll over, fat white muthafucker, where's your money?" I rolled over into the barrel of a .44 Magnum revolver pointed right between my eyes.

When I saw that gun, my survival instinct took over. I pointed to the cash. He searched through my stuff, left my clothes, took my bass and money, tied us up and left.

What happened was the gangsters had found out where we were and decided to give the punks a lesson and rip us off. Michael and Buddy, with single rooms, didn't open their doors and escaped the attack. They didn't come out of their rooms until the police left. So the whole band, with two exceptions, were tied up. The black members of the band got Uncle Tom lectures and the dealers took all their money, clothes, wigs and, for the coup de grace, stole the van with the instruments.

So there we were, hog-tied in our beds with all our possessions gone, humiliated and not knowing what's next when Detroit's finest arrive. The hole the junkies put us in kept getting deeper. The detectives left us tied up while we were being questioned. They refused to untie us until those responsible gave them the information that they needed.

Finally, they released us from our rope-and-duct-tape bonds

with a warning to get out of town. We called Grossman, who then arranged for our plane tickets back to New York. We had no money, no clothes, no instruments and our tails were firmly tucked between our legs.

I was a kid from Queens seeing and experiencing things I never knew existed before my San Francisco adventure and joining The Electric Flag. I remember sitting in a room with some of the band junkies talking music. As we talked, I'd see them nod off. I knew they were making me responsible for their lives. They would overdose and count on me and the others to get them to the gig on time. They were always wanting to borrow a few dollars. It got old, fast.

Michael left The Electric Flag because of his drug problems, which affected his playing and our touring. His original vision for the band was to play and create original music influenced by musicians that he personally respected. Instead, the band had become all about drugs and alcohol.

As Michael began to fall back into his basic "I only play the blues" thought process, Buddy started to push to take over. Michael was inspirational to play with, but he didn't want to leave his blues. I remember one day the great guitarist Larry Coryell came over to Michael's house while I was there. Larry, who was later known as the "Godfather of Fusion," was playing at the Fillmore. He wanted to share with Michael some new chords and fingerings he'd worked out, but Michael was not interested. By now, drugs had taken over Michael's life. He said, "I just want to play da blues."

We did a second album, this time without Michael. Buddy had taken over the band and was becoming more self-centered, with a maniacal, criminal attitude. There was some really good music on the album, but Buddy was starting to become unhinged. In my opinion, Nick Gravenites and myself were the only relatively sane ones left in the band.

With all of these problems blocking our creativity, The Electric Flag faded into history. Buddy went on to have success with his own band, the Buddy Miles Express, and then Santana and Jimi Hendrix's Band of Gypsys before succumbing to ill health brought on by drugs and his criminal behavior. He went to jail for grand theft in 1970 and later for auto theft in the early 1980s. We kept in touch and played one last time on a gig in New York City at the release party at B.B. King's Club for a documentary film on Jimi Hendrix. The Electric Flag became another classic blow-up story in the archives of sex, drugs and rock n' roll!

CHAPTER 9

The Bass Player's Job

1968: The Tet offensive begins — and becomes the turning point in the Vietnam War.

The bass player's job is to anchor the rhythm pattern and establish the harmony of the music. Being a self-taught musician, all of my schooling came from being in the moment, playing on a bandstand where most of the players were more experienced. As I progressed, more and more opportunities to play came my way. By learning established bass lines from the current hits of the day, I gained a valuable vocabulary of what to play and when. The bass, along with the drummer's bass drum pattern, provide the pulse — or heartbeat — to the music.

Growing up, I listened and learned from jazz bass players like Charles Mingus, Paul Chambers, Ray Brown, Ron Carter and Scott LaFaro, as well as R&B bass players like James Jamerson, Duck Dunn, Chuck Rainey and Gordon Edwards. These players shaped the sound and feel for the bass lines that I have created.

In music, harmony is the playing of three or more related notes simultaneously. Sometimes one person alone — such as a guitarist or pianist — creates this harmony. Other times several people, such as in an orchestra, jazz or rock band, create the harmony together. The bass plays a dominant role in how we hear these harmonies. When several notes are played at the same time, we hear them all

97

relative to the lowest sounding pitch — the bass note. So, along with providing the rhythmic heartbeat of the song, the bass can play notes that connect the chords or harmonies.

I noted that most electric bass players plucked the strings with their fingers — not a pick. I didn't have a method at that time; in fact, I wasn't even thinking about technique. I assumed that playing with your fingers was the right way to do it. And bass players I listened to and liked — like James Jamerson at Motown — also used their fingers. That was good enough for me.

All of their music was on the edge, a little behind the beat, so I learned to do it that way too. I like using my fingers because I feel the string, the tension and vibration of what I'm playing. I'm not really listening to myself, but I'm listening to the music going on around me. Behind the beat is tension. With the pick, I think it's more of an articulate, precise attack on the strings. Whether you use your fingers or a pick and are behind or in front of the beat, these techniques help to express the music. I try to use whatever technique the music asks for.

After my first bass instrument, I acquired a Rickenbacker, then a hollow-body blond Epiphone and finally a Fender Precision bass. Later, I gravitated back and forth between Fender Precision and Jazz basses. In the 1980s, at a music store in Red Bank, New Jersey, while playing in Clarence Clemons' Red Bank Rockers band, I found a Fender "A" Precision neck, which is rare. It is the smallest precision neck, but still slightly wider than the Jazz neck. I added a "PJ" set-up, using EMG Precision and Jazz-style pickups.

My preferred Fender neck is maple. That type of wood has flaws in it that gives me the sound I like. All necks have sonic characteristics. I found mine. I'm always looking for the right instrument for the right part.

I'm not really a collector. All of my instruments are basically tools to get the sounds that I want. As ideas and sounds develop or expand, I add them to my palette.

For example, I have a fretless bass made for me by Tom Gardner with a Macasser Ebony fingerboard on a two-piece maple neck that gives me the sound and feel of an upright bass. It's just there. I can really control the sound of it. On the road now, I use my fretless TG and my precision PJ and a Hartke LH1000 bass amp with two XL cabinets. When I began playing, I used an Ampeg B-15 amplifier. I found that on the road it wasn't loud enough, so I moved to two Fender Showman amps. With the Fabulous Rhinestones, I used Ampeg SVTs.

Over the years, I have had opportunities to work and play with some top guns. A few have been kind enough to share some of our history together. I think they offer a key to what I brought to their music.

During the *Soft Parade* sessions with The Doors, I was reacting to John Densmore on the drums. I first met him in the studio, and we had a very straight-on musician relationship. From my perspective, the drummer has to present me with a world of time, and it has to make sense. When he's in that world of time, we are both speaking the same language. I can go back and forth with him because I know his time is there. He told me that the band wanted to bring a jazzy, soulful sound to the album and explained my work on the session this way:

"It was a period of turbulence and distrust within The Doors — a time when the band recorded at different times of the day," Densmore told Frank Beacham in one of the interviews for this book. "Harvey's presence was like a rock during that session. Jim weighed a couple of hundred pounds and was drinking more and more. We had to do many more takes to get the vocals, which were primarily overdubbed. We laid down the tracks with Harvey, and Jim would sing scratch vocals. But they got along well. It was just heaven.

"To bass players and drummers, the space between each beat is long. If you emphasize the front of the beat, you are kind of playing military music. If you emphasize the back of the beat, then it's the blues. That's the feel of the whole thing. The Doors on *The Soft Parade* were somewhere in the middle of that beat. The bass player and the drummer have to feel the groove the same or you haven't got the pocket and the pocket is everything.

"At four bars in, Harvey and I were smiling at each other. Because we knew this is going to work. 'Touch Me' has this drum, tom tom stuff. Harvey's feel basically is a little bit back. It's almost blues. Not quite the blues, but it's back there. That's what I love. It makes the feel of music funky. Sort of like, 'Oh my God, is he going to play the next note on time? Oh, he made it! That's great!' It's that kind of thing.

"Also, Harvey played the bass with his fingers. Doug Lubahn, who worked on parts of the album, plays bass with a pick. Paul McCartney plays bass with a pick. It's cool, but it's not dirty enough for me. Jaco Pastorius plays electric bass with his fingers. It's like 'wow.' It's almost like a guitar the way he plays. You get more into it when your fingers are plucking on the string rather than click, click, click from a pick, pick, pick. I'm not putting McCartney down. He's one of the greatest songwriters of all time and a really great bass player. Especially his basslines, but the sound and the feel — I prefer Harvey. It's more black. It's more funky.

"Larry Graham was Sly Stone's bass player. He invented this popping sound on the bass. A real funky plucking with his fingers. The minute you hear it you know it's Sly. That's with the fingers."

I knew exactly what Densmore wanted. He created the basic rhythm pattern and feel for the song expecting me to incorporate his direction into my bass part. Ray's keyboard and Robbie's guitar parts filled out the rest of the song which allowed me to connect the bridges to the different sections in my bassline while staying out of the way of Jim's vocal phrasing.

My good friend, John Sebastian, who I played with on his album *John B. Sebastian*, added this: "Harvey's a good guy to have around when you need creative input to get out of a musical dilemma. Sometimes he can get you out of a fix because you didn't know you could do 2-5-1 just as easily as you could go 4-5-1.

"Also, there's a lot to Harvey's personality. He is good with the skittishness on the part of some musicians who have drug or personality problems. No matter how skittish they are, they quickly get the idea. Oh right, this guy is dependable on every take — not just the first two and then he loses concentration. They would see him as a kind of rock of quality. You couldn't move him off the time once it was dictated what the time was. That's how it was going to be. Harvey's steadiness is very important to these people."

David Bennett Cohen, a New York City-born musician who began in the club scene in the early 1960s, has been a friend since our earliest performing days. As a member of Country Joe and the Fish, beginning in December 1965, his group often shared the bill with The Electric Flag in the San Francisco Bay area and both groups played at the Monterey Pop Festival in 1967.

"Harvey is a highly evolved person," Cohen said. "As a bass player, he holds everything together. I personally think the bass is the most important instrument in the band because it's the bridge between pure rhythm and chords. It unites everything. Musically, Harvey held it together.

"His personality, however, is unique and definitely comes into his bass playing. No matter how technically good a musician is, personality means a lot. Take Jerry Garcia. There were guitar players who could play rings around him as far as technique goes. But when

Jerry played, his charisma came shining through. I think that's a beautiful thing. It is the same with Harvey, though Harvey is more of a background guy. His charisma comes through, but it really supports the whole band. That's how he is. It was apparent to everybody he played with. Harvey even got along with Dylan.

"He gives a level of confidence to the other musicians, but he also makes everyone in the band sound good. I know a lot of musicians, and some are great, but the best ones know how to play ensemble...they know how to make the ensemble sound more important than the individual player. Harvey really has that. That's one of the problems with many bands. I don't know the interworking of The Doors, but I suspect there was a lot of ego going on there. That kind of thing destroys unity and ensemble playing. Harvey was able to pull it together for those guys."

Cohen recalled that some other bands, especially the Paul Butterfield Blues Band, didn't think much of the musicianship of Country Joe and the Fish. "We were all friends, but it was very competitive," he said. "People like Elvin Bishop and others in the Butterfield group would sort of laugh when you mentioned Country Joe and the Fish. It was like we were a joke. Harvey, on the other hand, never, never treated anybody like that. He always showed complete respect. One day I was playing guitar at somebody's house and Harvey said now I know why Country Joe and the Fish is so successful. It was nice thing for him to say. That separates Harvey from the others."

CHAPTER 10

My Bass-Playing Influences

1968: Rev. Martin Luther King, Jr., civil rights leader, is assassinated in Memphis.

Charles Mingus

In his autobiography, *Beneath the Underdog*, Charlie Mingus begins with this quote:

> *"In other words I am three. One man stands forever in the middle, unconcerned, unmoved, watching, waiting to be allowed to express what he sees to the other two. The second man is like a frightened animal that attacks for fear of being attacked. Then there's an over-loving gentle person who lets people into the utmost sacred temple of his being and he'll take insults and be trusting and sign contracts without reading them and get talked down to working cheap or for nothing and when he realizes what has been done to him he feels like killing and destroying everything around him including himself for being so stupid. But he can't – he goes back inside himself."*

Have you ever heard Mingus' tune, "Fables of Faubus"? He expresses his disgust for Arkansas Governor Orval Faubus' racist attitudes with sarcastic bitter humor.

In the mid-1970s, I was living in Woodstock, New York, which had become a musical magnet for musicians. Master bassist and composer Charles Mingus had come to town to explore the possibility of buying a house in my neighborhood.

I got a call from Jack DeJohnette to see if Mingus could borrow my upright bass so he could play a gig at the Joyous Lake, a small music club in town. It was an honor beyond honors to have one of my main inspirations play my bass.

The sad thing for me was that I couldn't be at the club to hear him play because I had another gig. My upright bass was returned to me after the weekend gig with a note from Mingus with his thanks, saying he was sorry we did not get to meet in person.

In the 1960s, I got turned on to Mingus when I heard disc jockey Mort Fega play "Fables of Faubus" late at night on jazz radio station WEVD. The album, *Charles Mingus Presents Charles Mingus*, with Mingus' seething dialog and humorous interplay with his musicians, especially drummer Danny Richmond, grabbed my ears and introduced me to the role of bass player/composer.

The way Mingus and Richmond played off of each other is as good as it gets. Mingus' music is church gone blues and funk on the way to freedom. I like the way that it feels. My cultural roots are different, but the song comes from the same place.

Scott LaFaro

I discovered bassist Scott LaFaro on the album, *Waltz for Debby* by the Bill Evans Trio recorded live at the Village Vanguard. All the bass players I was familiar with at that time — Paul Chambers, Sam Jones and Ray Brown — laid in the pocket, keeping the feel or groove solid. They created a foundation for all the other instruments to have melodic movement.

I didn't realize it at the time, but Scott LaFaro's counter-melodic style created the three equal voices in a trio concept, collectively working together organically towards a singular musical idea, often without the time being explicitly stated. LaFaro's prodigious technique on bass made this concept possible.

Listening to LaFaro's playing helped me to expand my melodic approach and probably influenced Jack Bruce, bassist for the British rock band, Cream, in his trio playing with Clapton. The idea of the bass in whatever form — electric or acoustic — having an equal say in the music comes from Scott LaFaro.

Milt Hinton

When I first listened to Cab Calloway, I didn't know I was listening to the solid rhythmic bass playing of Milt Hinton. By osmosis, Milt was my first bass teacher. His mission was to lay down a solid foundation for the rest of the band and go to the 4/4 walk for the solos. Milt knew all about the comfortable notes and rhythms that free the soloist and let the band swing.

After traveling and thriving for many years, big orchestras began to go out of style with the arrival of World War II. Trying to conserve resources, the bands gradually got smaller and smaller. By the beginning of the early 1950s, most had gone bankrupt or were calling it quits. Milt's career on the road was mostly over.

Back in New York City, Milt picked up local gigs and eventually became a session musician. He was the epitome of the studio session player and could fit into any genre. Starting in the mid-1950s, Milt was part of a rhythm section that included Hank Jones (piano), Barry Galbraith (guitar) and Osie Johnson (drums) playing together on hundreds of records. They even recorded their own album, *The Rhythm*

Section.

Until 1970, Milt recorded with everyone from Billie Holiday to Paul McCartney, Frank Sinatra to Leon Redbone and Sam Cooke to Barbra Streisand. Milt summarized his time in the studios: "I might be on a date for Andre Kostelanetz in the morning, do one with Brook Benton or Johnny Mathis in the afternoon, and then finish up the day with Paul Anka or Bobby Rydell."

In addition to being a great musician, Milt Hinton was also a master photographer. Between 1935 and 1999, he took thousands of photographs — about 60,000 of them in all. His work shows many great artists on the road, in studios and at home. It also captured the racial segregation of the time and became a vivid document of what black musicians had to endure on the road. A number of books of Milt's photographs have been published.

In 1989, when Bonnie and I got married, she invited her friend, Doris Elliot, the wife of vibraphonist Don Elliot, to our wedding. Don had passed away a few years earlier. Doris had told Milt about our wedding and, as a gift, he sent along one of his books, *The Stories and Photographs of Milt Hinton*. Inside, Milt inscribed "Best wishes for a long and happy marriage."

Ron Carter

During the *Bitches Brew* sessions with Miles Davis, I got a call on November 19, 1969 to go to Columbia's Studio E. That was the day I got to meet and play with Ron Carter on the tune, "Great Expectations." He was and is a major influence in my playing and on how important supporting the melody and rhythm is to quality music. It's what makes the music feel good.

Carter's work is included with Miles Davis on *Seven Steps to Heaven* and *Miles Smiles* along with Tony Williams (drums) and

Herbie Hancock (piano). His recorded albums with Herbie Hancock (*Maiden Voyage*) and McCoy Tyner (*The Real McCoy*) are some of the quintessential examples of how it's done.

James Jamerson

Playing Motown, The Beatles and Rolling Stones tunes in cover bands was the backbone of my gigs in the 1960s. Motown had the most hits of the era. I, like so many other musicians, learned from James Jamerson's amazing bass lines on "Bernadette," "I Was Made to Love Her," "I'm Wondering", "What's Going On" and many, many more.

Jamerson was the artist I spent hours listening to and marveling at his note selection. He opened up the world of the electric bass controlling and directing harmony and rhythm.

Duck Dunn

I met Duck Dunn at the Monterey Pop Festival in 1967. He was there to perform with Otis Redding. I told him I was with The Electric Flag and he smiled. I don't think he had heard of the band or me but acknowledged my existence anyway.

The conversation was mostly me telling Duck how cool I thought his bass parts were on "Born under a Bad Sign," "Green Onions" and "Soul Man." I told him how his music was the inspiration for my basslines with the Flag.

I later ran into Duck in Atlanta and asked him if he remembered our conversation backstage at Monterey Pop. He said no, but by then at least he was familiar with my playing.

Chuck Rainey

In 1967, as far as studio work was concerned, Chuck Rainey was doing most of the R&B sessions and I was doing most of the folk-rock sessions. On some days, I'd have three or four recording sessions lined up.

While waiting in the lounge at A&R Studios for the second session of the day, my friend recording engineer Shelly Yakus, invited me into the control room to check out the recording bass player. That was the first time I'd heard Chuck Rainey, who was playing with the aforementioned drummer Bernard Purdie. They blew my socks off!

Chuck's many great basslines that have become virtual clichés include Aretha Franklin's *Amazing Grace*, Marvin Gaye's *I Want You*, Steely Dan's *Pretzel Logic*, Donald Fagen's solo album *The Nightfly*, and of course the work of Quincy Jones.

CHAPTER 11

Super Session

1968: Robert F. Kennedy assassinated in Los Angeles.

Al Kooper had just taken a new job as a producer at Columbia Records. He was anxious to prove himself in the job and needed a high-profile concept for his first recording at the label. He thought back to the great jazz formula of stating the melody of the tune and then improvising on it. It was that simple. He had come up with his  hook. Jazz or jam musicians essentially ad-lib with each other — speaking in a musical language. Al brought his improvisational jazz influences into blues-rock.

The musicians listen not to themselves, but to what's going on around them. Each player reacts to it. There are two phases in the process. In the first, the player gets comfortable with the rhythm and chord changes. This becomes the vocabulary of the song. In the second phase, the conversation begins. The musicians listen to each other, reacting to what they hear by playing what they feel.

It takes a strong leader to give this concept direction. To pull it off, Kooper hired Mike Bloomfield to play guitar and me to play bass. Bloomfield suggested drummer Eddie Hoh and Barry Goldberg for piano. Kooper handled the vocals and played some piano, organ, ondioline (an early electronic keyboard), electric guitar and 12-string guitar.

We recorded in May 1968, over two days in Studio A at the historic CBS Columbia Square on Sunset Boulevard in Hollywood. The building housed many of the Golden Age radio shows, the early CBS television network and the Nestor Film Company, the first motion picture studio in Hollywood. Bob Dylan, Barbra Streisand and many other top stars recorded albums in this studio. We were next.

Two days before I left for Hollywood to do the session, I was sitting on the porch of my house at 35 Carmelita Street in Mill Valley enjoying a mellow afternoon with my then girlfriend, Mary.

I met Mary in Boston in the Fort Hills section of Roxbury at a party with the Jim Kweskin Jug Band. She had just broken up with her boyfriend and one thing led to another and I woke up the next morning with Mary in a bedroom at Mel Lyman's communal house. Mel was the harmonica player in Kweskin's band, but he became something of a cult leader, heading the Fort Hill Community before his death in 1978. I got my shit together and had to get back to the hotel I was staying at to leave for the next gig. When I said goodbye, Mary asked if she flew to Mill Valley where I was living could she visit me. I said sure, just call first.

I was in Boston playing with Electric Flag at the Psychedelic Supermarket. The venue was a converted parking garage, with acoustic qualities to match, and it was not remembered fondly by bands or patrons.

One of the highlights of that gig was while doing a soundcheck Marcus Doubleday, our trumpet player, passed out playing the intro to "Groovin' is Easy" and fell face first off a 10-foot high stage. We picked him up off the floor and as we took him to the dressing room, he assured us he was okay because he was feeling no pain as our road manager wiped the blood and stopped the bleeding.

So Mary flew out to San Francisco and visited for a day or two then moved in. It was a relationship of convenience. It was never a love affair. We were in Like!

We had a visit from Goldfinger, a friend from Haight Ashbury, who brought a psychedelic gift for us to try. It was blue psilocybin mushrooms.

I was already familiar with Owsley Stanley's LSD (a/k/a "acid"), having been dosed with it at The Fillmore in San Francisco at an Electric Flag gig. I told Goldfinger I had to be at a session in LA in two days and asked how long the stuff lasted. He said no more than 10 to 12 hours. Needless to say, that wasn't even close to being true. Mary and I were up for 48 hours, hallucinating and counting the molecules in the ceiling above our heads.

My friend Richard Greene, a violinist, was staying with us at the time while he rehearsed with his new band, Seatrain. He returned to the house around 3:30 a.m., finding me on an inspection tour of all the objects and artwork on the tables and walls. He suggested we play chess. I immediately sat down at the chessboard and we launched into a chess frenzy. He later told me it was the most spiritual chess match he had ever played.

When I met Bloomfield for the flight to Los Angeles, I was wearing sunglasses to hide my eyes, since I was still coming down from the psilocybin. I was not really prepared for the scene at the airport, when Bloomfield was told that he could not take his guitar on board. At first, he tried being nice. When that didn't work, he tried the "get me the manager" ploy. Meanwhile, I had my bass in a hard travel case, putting it onto the conveyor belt with the rest of the baggage, still trying to cool Michael down. Finally, a compromise was reached. Michael was able to store his guitar in the suit bag compartment and we boarded the plane.

When we landed in Los Angeles, we went our separate ways. Michael was staying with Al in a rented house, and I was booked into the Landmark Motor Hotel at 7047 Franklin Avenue in Hollywood, the place where Janis Joplin would overdose on heroin a couple of years later. The session was at night and I was totally energized by the time the first of our encounters was scheduled to start. I left the hotel, taking a cab to the studio.

The psilocybin was just about out of my system as I walked through the studio doors. Al greeted me from the recording console, sharing his creative vision for the album. It sounded good to me. With his direction taken, I walked into Studio A.

The session man, Eddie Hoh, was setting up his drums for the session when I approached and introduced myself. As we talked, he was setting up and tuning his drum kit. I could tell that this was going to be good. I could hear it — his tuning was musical. Each drum was in tune with the other drums leaving space in the sound spectrum for my bass line. I knew then that our chemistry would work.

The session started and went flawlessly. The music just started to flow. We were all comfortable with each other. When Bloomfield was on, he had an infectious energy that would spread outward to everyone in the room. He was contagious.

When Mike, Barry and I played together in The Electric Flag there would be this lock, where everyone would be in sync and the real joy of the music would rise to the top. We got that same feeling, only better, in the CBS studio that night. It was all caught on the tape.

The first tune we did was "Albert's Shuffle," written by Kooper and Bloomfield. I believe it was named for Dylan's manager, Albert Grossman, who was always shuffling his deck of artists and players to see what made the best band or hand.

The tempo was about 67 on the metronome. Good shuffle feel.

Next, Bloomfield came up with a Howard Tate song, "Stop," written by Jerry Ragovoy. We had messed around with it at Flag rehearsals, but never figured out the bridge. In this version, we used the verse and chorus and jammed using the bassline as the theme lick. Al added horns to help lock in the feel.

The first vocal was a Curtis Mayfield song, "Man's Temptation." Al is no Curtis Mayfield as a singer, but he went for it. Next up, "His Modal Majesty," was the band searching for a groove and then finding it while Al experimented with a new instrument he acquired called the ondioline. It was a forerunner of today's synthesizers invented in 1941 by the Frenchman Georges Jenny. We ended the evening's session with a classic slow blues tune, "Really." We all left Studio A, looking forward to our next day. There had been no drama or distractions at the session.

The drama would come on day two. None of us ever knew what was cooking in Bloomfield's mental kitchen. Sometime during the night, Bloomfield got up, packed up his stuff, snuck out of Al's house and went back home to Mill Valley. He left Al a note saying, "Couldn't sleep. Went home. Sorry." It became a nightmare for Al! With half the album recorded and the rest of us all in place to finish it the next day, Bloomfield's abrupt departure left Kooper in a major predicament. To me, it was a disaster.

Of course, what Bloomfield did was not a surprise to me. I had gotten used to his erratic behavior from past performances with the Flag and knew him pretty well. Bloomfield had his own priorities and he didn't really care about anyone else. He was — to put it kindly — a charming asshole. If he didn't sleep or get the drugs he needed, he would do whatever he needed to do to feel better. He did this throughout his erratic career. But we all loved him!

The success or failure of the recording was now all on Kooper's shoulders, who rose to the occasion and solved the problem in a brilliant way. He picked up the phone and hired Stephen Stills, the then-guitarist for Buffalo Springfield, to play on side two of the record. I was familiar with Stills and Buffalo Springfield's material, but this was the first time I had played with him. Kooper was the driving force leading us through tunes he selected.

Just as there was magic the night before, that magic reappeared in a slightly different form with the fluid guitar playing of Stills. In looking back, Bloomfield's action and Kooper's response to it turned the album into the classic it is today.

Al came up with his own arrangement for Dylan's "It Takes a Lot to Laugh, It Takes a Train to Cry," which featured his vocals and Stills' guitar solos with my aggressive bassline to move it along. Al and I had recorded this tune for Dylan on the *Highway 61 Revisited* album. This kind of warmed us up for "Season of the Witch" and an arrangement Donovan would never have thought of.

As I remember it, Stills was playing around with his wah-wah pedal and we kind of fell in with him. After learning the song while jamming, Kooper started singing and it took off. I don't think we did many takes. We recorded three tunes that night, but still needed one more to finish the record. Kooper asked if anybody had anything. I said, "Yeah, I've got something."

I played "Harvey's Tune" and sang the melody for the group. I had written it while playing with the folk duo Jim and Jean. I stayed at the home of Jean's mother in Malibu Beach when we played the Ash Grove in Santa Monica. There were no lyrics — just chords and a melody.

At that same house, I met Jean's brother, Brian Ray, who now plays guitar in Paul McCartney's band. He was about eight years old at the time and had liked the tune. Kooper and the others liked it too. So we recorded it as the last song of the night. Kooper and Joey Scott's arrangement with horns back in New York City helped

"Harvey's Tune" reach its full potential.

In two days, *Super Session* was finished. Only some overdubbing was left, which would be done later in New York City. The album was released in May 1968, less than two months later. It cost $13,000 to make. The record peaked at #12 on the Billboard 200 and went on to become a huge hit. It was later certified gold. Super Session still sells more than 50 years later and was re-released in 2014 in a higher-quality, 5.1 channel SACD version.

In my opinion, the success of *Super Session* opened the door for the "supergroup" recording concept of the late 1960s and 1970s — Blind Faith, Crosby, Stills and Nash and the like. A key reason for the success was the intervention of the fickle finger of fate — in the form of Bloomfield leaving after recording one side of the album and Kooper bringing in Stephen Stills for the second side. It gave the recording a diversity that it needed to become a classic. No one could have foreseen this, but Bloomfield's exit and Stills walking in the door created a classic gold record.

Kooper has also said, and I wholeheartedly agree, that the record was successful because none of the musicians had anything at stake artistically when they went into it. It was not a project on anyone's map. It just happened. It was a "playing" thing. That's the element that made those great jazz sessions work.

But only a leader with Al's genius could have put something like this together. We just played and it worked.

CHAPTER 12

Strangers in the Night

1968: Police violence breaks out at the Democratic National Convention as the world watches on live television.

From day one of my journey from local to pop musician after my Bob Dylan session, women attracted to the bright lights and excitement played a very important role in my career. Being unmarried and a free agent, these very friendly women added warmth and pleasure to my travels. I can't imagine what I'd be called in today's "Me Too" world, but it was the 1960s — a different time and a different place. The slogan "sex, drugs and rock n' roll" was extremely apropos.

A Night at the Fillmore

I came from a pretty straight background before the Dylan session. Sure, I had smoked some reefer but that was about it. Then I moved to Mill Valley, north of San Francisco over the Golden Gate Bridge, as part of a new super group, soon to be named The Electric Flag.

Part of the initiation into the San Francisco music scene was going to the Fillmore Auditorium to see and hear Janis Joplin, the Grateful Dead or Jefferson Airplane. So, Buddy Miles and I, being the uninitiated newcomers to the scene, borrowed the beat-up blue Ford van and headed downtown over the Golden Gate Bridge to the corner of Fillmore and Geary streets. We walked from one-dimensional reality into a new reality, with light projections on the walls. Behind the stage, there was Day-Glo paint on the floor. Buddy went his way and I went mine. The Grateful Dead was playing that night. While it was not my chosen music for some mysterious reason, I quickly got into it. The floor was filled with women gracefully dancing free form. I'm sure my mood was influenced by the coke I'd taken, spiked with Owsley acid.

Just as I felt this tingly warmth start to come on, I noticed that one of the dancers was glancing over in my direction. I was wearing a leather jacket, Levi's, white tee shirt, Tony Lama boots and dark glasses. She was barefoot and had Day-Glo face paint. She was wearing a black leotard, a crown of leaves, a pale yellow chiffon blouse and had many loose necklaces draped around her neck.

I walked over to her, we began gyrating in a psychedelic-inspired dance marathon that lasted till Jerry Garcia left the stage and the party ended. Up until this time, we had not spoken a word. I took the initiative and told her about the new super group I was in and who I had recorded and performed with. She gave me a long look and grabbed my hand as she led me out of the Fillmore into a cab that took us down a long winding street.

The street had eight hair-pinned turns that had my psychedelically-saturated brain reeling and then finally dropping us off at her apartment on Lombard and Hyde streets. As we walked into the apartment, she spoke her first words to me: "My name is Miss Sweetie and I will be sweet to you."

Backstage at Major Rock Venues

Being a sideman when I performed with The Doors, I didn't have the opportunities Jim Morrison or any of the other principal band members had when we played places like the Los Angeles Forum or New York's Madison Square Garden. Those front-line players got to meet the upper groupie echelon of fashion models, wealthy women or stars in their own right. The women I would meet at the show would usually be too shy, not sexy enough or too late for the top guns. So I played it cool and waited. I was sitting in the Doors dressing room after our show at Madison Square Garden sipping on a vodka and cranberry juice when a long pointed, silver finger-nailed hand lightly touched my shoulder. "Are you the bass player?"

I said yes, I was he and who might you be? "I'm Cheryl. Jim said I should come over and meet you because you're famous and you recorded with Bob Dylan. I just love him too."

She was dressed in fringed doe-skinned boots with a see-through blouse, no bra, three strands of beads and the aromatic mood-setting fragrance of patchouli oil. It was lust at first sight. She asked if I wanted to smoke a joint. I suggested we continue the conversation in the private bathroom.

As soon as we got into the bathroom, she lit up a joint and handed it to me. Then she dropped to her knees, pulled my pants zipper down and lit up my joint as I leaned back against the sink. We finished smoking, she giggled, said goodbye, and was gone in minutes.

The Continuing Party Around Jimi Hendrix

Wherever Jimi Hendrix went, there was a party around him. This time, I had just finished a rehearsal at the Bitter End where The Electric Flag was playing and was walking down Bleecker Street over to Gem Spa on Second Avenue to get an egg cream and a pretzel. A long black Caddy limo pulled up next to me and it was Jimi with his entourage. He opened the door and asked, "Want a ride?"

I looked inside the limo and saw Jimi with three gorgeous women, all of whom must have been models. I couldn't resist, so I jumped in. It was about six o'clock and Jimi and the ladies were going to dinner at the Chelsea Hotel. I told him where I was going and Jimi said, "No man, you're coming with us."

I squeezed in between two of the young ladies and being the perfect host, Jimi made the introductions. "Monique, Suella and Brandy, this is Harvey, we go way back to the beginning together."

Arriving at the Chelsea, we had a table waiting for us. The one thing I had to keep in mind was that I had to be at my gig at the Bitter End by 9:30 p.m. at the latest. By the sheerest of coincidences, the ladies were also staying at the Chelsea. So, after gorging on clams on the half shell and drinking Johnny Walker Red with beer chasers, we went upstairs. I looked at my watch and it was 7:30. I figured if I was out of there by nine, I'd be good for the gig.

After some suggestive conversation, Brandy invited me into the bedroom. At 8:15, I glanced at my watch, jumped out of bed, got dressed and made it to the gig at the Bitter End just in time to make the downbeat.

CHAPTER 13

The Soft Parade

1968: President Johnson announces he will not seek or accept the presidential renomination.

In May 1968, I was in Los Angeles with The Electric Flag. We played the Whiskey a Go Go in Hollywood and the Cheetah Club in Venice. At the Cheetah, I was on stage with the band playing an Otis Redding tune, "I'm Sick Y'All." As the ending chorus began repeating, the groove between Buddy and I got deeper and deeper. Suddenly, this guy comes on stage dancing and tripping around, finally falling at my feet. He then proceeded to slobber on my sandaled toes.

Backstage, after the show, I met Robbie Krieger, guitarist for The Doors. I made a sarcastic remark about the drunk lying at my feet on the stage. Krieger informed me the drunk was the lead singer of his band.

"Well, we all have our moments," I responded. That was my introduction to Jim Morrison.

Robbie and I shared similar influences in music. It was he who invited me out to Malibu to jam with The Doors later that week. There I met keyboard player, Ray Manzarek, whose left hand was the band's usual bass player. In the jam, Ray gave me plenty of room to be creative and to lock in with John Densmore's drums.

Playing with Densmore was a totally different experience than playing with Buddy Miles. His groove was tight, musical and thoughtful, while Buddy's was powerful and emotional.

After a couple of hours of playing, we went to hang out on the beach at Malibu and I met up with the front man, singer Jim Morrison. Jim was jokingly apologetic about the Cheetah Club and said, "We must do that again sometime, when I'm sober!"

Outside of the live gigs with The Electric Flag, I was in LA on other projects. Staying at the Chateau Marmont Hotel on the Sunset Strip in Hollywood, I was 10 minutes from the new Elektra Studios on La Cienega Boulevard and 15 minutes from Wally Heider's Studio, where I was working with producer John Simon on Cass Elliot's solo album, *Dream a Little Dream*. John and I were also co-producing the second Electric Flag album for Columbia Records.

One evening, I was at a pool party at the Laurel Canyon home of Peter Tork, guitar player for the Monkees. It featured naked groupies and jamming musicians including Jimi Hendrix, Stephen Stills, Buddy Miles and Joni Mitchell. After the party, when I returned to the hotel, I received a phone call from Paul Rothchild, the producer of the Doors, who wanted to meet with me to talk about a new album project. It was to be called *The Soft Parade*.

I had met Rothchild two years earlier backstage at the Café Au Go Go in New York through Paul Butterfield, whose work he had also produced. Rothchild was familiar with my work and liked me because I have a funky kind of feel to my playing. Our meeting was at Rothchild's home in Laurel Canyon with my good friend Paul Harris, the arranger/keyboardist.

I learned there that I had been given a thumbs up by Densmore and Krieger after our jam. Both felt secure with my sound. I suspected that Rothchild had engineered that meeting with The Doors members at the Cheetah Club and the subsequent jam as a tryout. However, as our discussion went on, Rothchild told me there was a problem with *The Soft Parade* project — a big one. The band, he said, was in a negative state of mind and, as a result, their music was stale. In fact, Jim Morrison and the band's other members were barely on speaking terms. They were erratic and barely communicating at all. It was, he said, a dysfunctional band.

My job, Rothchild said, was to direct the music from the bass perspective to set up the rhythm tracks for Paul Harris' arrangements with horns and strings. I accepted the challenge and was immediately on board. Rothchild would call the next morning with our recording schedule.

October 1968

We recorded *The Soft Parade* at the new Elektra Studio on La Cienega Boulevard in Santa Monica. The studio — elegant and plush — had just been finished. It was fitted with Persian rugs and warm Indian pillows in red, orange and browns. All the instruments and amplifiers, which included an Ampeg B-15, Fender Bassman and an Acoustic 361 bass amp, were sitting on these rugs.

Beautiful wood paneling and the latest acoustic treatment surrounded the playing field. There were cushioned stools to sit on and state-of-the-art mixer controls for the headphones. In the control room, Bruce Botnick, the long-time sound engineer for The Doors, was manning the audio console.

Call time was 1 p.m. on the first day of the project, and I was there on time and ready to begin. But no other band members were at the studio. So I walked back into the control room, sat down and smoked a joint with Rothschild and Botnick while we waited for the band members to arrive.

By 3:30 p.m., all the band members — minus Jim Morrison — had assembled. The atmosphere was tense, and it took me awhile to find my comfort zone. I found it when we got down to the music. "Touch Me" was the first tune we worked on that day. Then came "Tell All the People," "Shaman's Blues," "Do It," "Runnin' Blue" and "The Soft Parade." My job at the session was to tie together the verse/chorus section dots with connecting bridges that would hold the track together, leaving space for the vocals as well as the horns and strings.

I was actually used to this method, having been hired for sessions in New York where we recorded having only a chord chart to follow. The songs were written from the basic tracks we put down. The first time I heard the "Touch Me" vocal was at the vocal session after the rhythm track was completed. If the reference vocal Morrison put on worked, we were done with that basic track. If not, we'd re-record it.

Paul Harris was doing the horn and string arrangements. After Jim put his reference vocal down, Paul would then do his arranging, working off the vocal, bass and drum pattern and harmonic structure of the keyboard and guitar. I put a bass track down that went with what Ray and Robbie had played and locked it all into John's drums so that we had a cohesive rhythm track for Morrison to sing over.

I was at the studio over a month, but we didn't do that much actual recording during those days. Though I would have a call time for each session, I usually had to wait for the rest of the band to arrive. They came in piecemeal, as individuals, at staggered times. As I waited, I'd hear Rothchild on the phone in the background, screaming to various band members that they were late. When everyone finally assembled, it was often very late in the day and we'd end up recording very short sessions.

Because of the band's dysfunction at that time, Rothchild had to go with the flow, as did the rest of the band. But until Morrison recorded the vocals, no one really knew what would work or not.

I had no problems with anyone. Yet my work with The Doors, including Morrison, was a real rollercoaster ride. If I had been a therapist, I would have been paid double time because of the fragmented egos of the band. Unlike working with Dylan, where we were in a tightly controlled environment, The Doors sessions were the opposite. We weren't doing complete performances. I did my job and tried to get musical satisfaction out of making tight tracks.

That said, the band members were professional, responsible people. They knew they had to deliver the project. Morrison, on the other hand, wasn't so concerned. He was still very angry and heavily into drugs and alcohol. My past experience with Mike Bloomfield had taught me to see situations from several different points of view.

Morrison wasn't worried about it because he thought he could do anything he wanted. To him, the rest of the group was like his backup band. When I say the band was broken at the time, I mean it was Morrison versus the other members. I knew it was my job to be a "rock" during the sessions and help create bridges in many of the songs.

Bill Siddons, manager of The Doors, explained the past history of the group's dynamic in the documentary *Feast of Friends*:

"One of the few times I saw Jim angry was when he found out about, 'come on Buick, Light My Fire.' Out of control. He felt betrayed. His partners had betrayed him, they had sold out to corporate America without asking him. I was there when he told them. 'How could you do this to me? This is my band too. How could you make that decision without me?'

"One of them answered, 'Well, man, you didn't tell us where you were going and the offer would have expired.'"

'So what?'

"Morrison just didn't get it. Whether he was gone for a day or a month, it didn't matter, but you don't sell out to the establishment. Postpone it or cancel, but don't give my soul away. That was the end of the dream. That was the end of that era of Jim's relationship with the other members of the band; from then on it was business. That was the day Jim said, 'I don't have partners anymore, I have associates.'"

Morrison only showed up at the studio to lay down his reference vocals. He recorded at night without his band mates. I would wait for a phone call from Paul Rothchild, letting me know that Morrison was in the studio and for me to come by.

I was surprised to see he came with his girlfriend, Pam Courson, who I knew from New York City. Pam was a dancer at the Eighth Wonder, one of the music bars I used to play at on Eight Street in New York's Greenwich Village. We used to hang out after hours. When I came to Morrison's late-night sessions, I spent most of the time talking to Pam.

When I said hello to Pam, I could not help but note how much she had changed. She had more money at her disposal; she was now Jim Morrison's girlfriend and had the status that came with it. He bought her a fashion boutique, which she operated in LA. They seemed to have a spark between them. She was with him until the very end.

One night, Rothchild called and said he was going to listen to some stuff with Jim. Did I want to come over?

Sitting on a comfy leather sofa in the control room with Jim and Paul, we listened to some of Jim's reference vocals. He asked me what I thought about each one we listened to, seeming to actually be interested in what I was saying. A bond had formed between us, and this bond would last through the LA Forum and Madison Square

Garden concerts, when I returned to Los Angeles.

With Jim Morrison at Madison Square Garden.
Photo courtesy of Joe Sia

I tried to speak with Morrison only when he was sober. In his drugged-out situations, I avoided him. For me, it was a waste of time to talk with him when he was stoned. Jim was a charismatic guy to hang with until Mr. Hyde appeared, then it was time for me to take my exit. Cleaning up his mess wasn't in my job description. Outside of his addiction, I felt Morrison simply had a business dispute with the band members and disagreed with the choice of some of the songs they selected for the album. He had a hard time singing some of them.

In my opinion, the unique sound of The Doors was created by Ray's keyboard style alongside Robbie's solid and melodic guitar parts. Jim was the voice, the poet/artist, the sex symbol that sold the band. When the band started making decisions based on business rather than artistic principle, it was essentially over.

Though *The Soft Parade*, for the most part, got terrible reviews, it was a financial success.

Rothchild was a merciless taskmaster who maintained quality control no matter what. He was a great producer and also a masterful manipulator. He was ultimately responsible for the final product and got what he needed from the band.

"Touch Me" was released first as a single in December 1968. Three additional singles from the album, "Wishful Sinful," "Tell All the People" and "Runnin' Blue" also became hits. *The Soft Parade* album was released on July 18, 1969 on the Elektra label. Despite a lukewarm critical reception featuring a cold shoulder from *Rolling Stone*, the album became the band's fourth Top 10 hit album in a row.

Densmore said that beyond *The Soft Parade* album itself, the project was an important turning point for the band. "I have this theory that *The Soft Parade* led us to the fifth and sixth albums, *Morrison Hotel* and *L.A. Woman*, which were done in our rehearsal studio in two takes and all done in a week like funky garage albums. If we hadn't gone through *The Soft Parade* experience and tried all the stuff we were interested in doing, we wouldn't have gotten back to the later albums. It was an important advance for us."

———

After the *Soft Parade* recording sessions were finished in November 1968, I was asked by the band's management to do two concerts with The Doors: one at The Forum in Inglewood, California on Dec. 14, 1968 and one at Madison Square Garden on Jan. 24, 1969. I would have a chance to see two distinctly different sides of The Doors at these concerts.

At The Forum, we had an audience of 18,000, a string sextet, a horn section and thirty-two amplifiers. There were three opening acts: Tzon Yen Luie, a Japanese koto player; the band Sweetwater; and Jerry Lee Lewis. All three were booed by the audience, prompting Lewis to tell the crowd: "I hope you all have a heart attack."

John Densmore said the band had picked Jerry Lee Lewis for the opening act and he was in his country phase at the time. However, Densmore recalled, we warned Lewis to do some of his old rock hits. Watching from the audience, Densmore said he loved every minute of Lewis' performance, even though half the audience simply didn't get it. He laughed, recalling that Lewis gave the audience the finger when he left the stage.

That was a precursor of what was to come next. When The Doors came on, we started playing the new material from *The Soft Parade*, though the album had not yet been released. A lot of the fans started chanting for old hits like "Light My Fire," which the band did not plan to do. The audience didn't want to hear the new songs. All they wanted were the old hits.

So Morrison started to get nasty with the audience. "Cut the shit!" he told them. "What are you all doing here?" He was starting on a path that would end up getting him arrested in Miami three months later. I was behind Morrison on the stage, watching him deal with his audience.

Any stage veteran knew he was doing the worst thing possible. He let the audience take over his concert and gave up — allowing his temper to rule the show. This was why he got into all those battles ahead. It was the first time I had ever witnessed that kind of breakdown on stage. Morrison just went all out. For me, it was like an out-of-body experience, since I had a firsthand view standing on the stage a few feet behind him.

Morrison then sat down for 10 or 15 minutes and read the lyrics to *The Celebration of the Lizard*. My reaction was I'm up here with The Doors and getting paid pretty well. The music was fine when we played. But I was just really watching the show. When it all ended, Morrison simply walked off the stage with no ovation. To put it politely, the performance was a disaster.

On Jan. 24, at Madison Square Garden, things were totally different. The opening act was the Staples Singers. It was a far larger venue and The Doors were getting $50,000, one of the largest fees paid to any rock band at the time.

Looking out at the audience, which filled the arena, was an

awesome experience. On stage, the buzz of the event was more powerful than the grounding buzz emanating from all of the amplifiers. The band was on fire.

Setlist

1. Touch Me
2. The Soft Parade
3. Tell All the People
4. Love Me Two Times
5. Who Scared You?
6. Spanish Caravan
7. Wild Child
8. Light My Fire

Encore

9. Back Door Man
10. Woman Is a Devil
11. Five to One
12. Adolph Hitler
13. When the Music's Over

It was a straight-ahead concert at the Garden. I was at my usual "view from the bottom" position, back by the drummer's hi-hat, connecting the band with the horn section. The monitors and overall sound system were relatively non-existent, so my concentration was aimed at being tight with Densmore so the section could get their timing from us and not have to depend on the stage monitors. Morrison was far more subdued and was having a good time while performing. It was cool playing "Light My Fire" with the band.

Even with the huge success of the Madison Square Garden concert, some critics sensed it was the beginning of the end for The

Doors. Morrison himself was aware of the dichotomies at one point during the concert when he pointed to one side of the arena and said, "You are life" and then pointing to the other side, he said, "You are death." Then, he added, "I straddle the fence, and my balls hurt."

After that night, I went to Los Angeles to resume other projects. It would be my last time performing with The Doors.

One footnote. After Morrison died at age 27, Pamela Courson came back to America from Europe and brought with her a collection of Morrison's poems and journals. Pam died on April 25, 1974, also at age 27, from a heroin overdose on a living room couch in a Los Angeles apartment that she shared with two male friends. After her death, "ownership" of Morrison's work changed hands and was offered for sale over a 12-year period by a parade of characters.

Since I had played with The Doors, I was offered a chance to buy a share in the material. However, the ownership and legitimacy of the material was in question and I passed. It was later published.

131

Early Professional Life

Purity! Idealism! Self expression!.. I was lucky - Right place, right time.

The Electric Flag at the Monterey Pop Festival, 1967.

Jamming with Jimi Hendrix at the Shrine Auditorium, Los Angeles, California, February 10, 1968. Photo by Gottlieb Walker.

What a Wonderful Thing We Have – Sheet Music.

My older sister Roberta and her friend Ruby took me to my
first rock 'n' roll show. Murray the K's Big Holiday show
at the Brooklyn Fox.

With Fred Neil and Mike Lang at the Grand Hotel Du Lac on Lake Geneva for the 9th International Montreux Festival 1975.

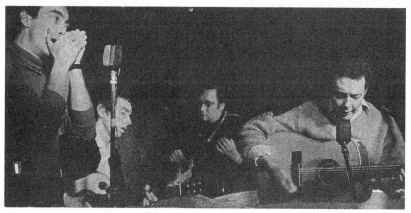

Left to Right: Oz Bach, John ?, Me and Fred Neil at the Cafe Au Go Go 1966.

Left to Right: Stew Cutler, Baron Raymonde, Angel Rissof, Me, Garry Bruer and Gary Brooks.

Me with Kal David at the Bearsville Theater in Woodstock.
Photo by Bonnie Brooks

Leon Russell, Karl Himmel, Robert Lee, and me in Atlanta 1979.

Lester Chambers and me.

Former Earth, Wind and Fire, Phil Collins horn section that
played with a 1980's version of the Electric Flag.

Bruce Springsteen jamming with Clarence Clemons' band The
Red Bank Rockers at Clemons' club Big Man's West 1981.
Photo courtesy of **Jack Scarangella.**

Me with Wavy Gravy in Tokyo Japan - Save the Whales concert.

Rehearsal at John Sebastian's house in Sag Harbor with Dallas Taylor

Last version of The Fabulous Rhinestones. L to R: Barry Jackson, Kal David, Eric Parker, Arti Funaro, Bob Lienbach, Gary Brooks

Me with Danny Louis, Gary Brooks, Lester Chambers, Gary Gold and unseen guitarist Stew Cutler

With the bass I loaned to Charlie Mingus

DEAR HARVEY BROOKS

THANKS VERY MUCH FOR
LETTING ME USE YOUR
BASS, SORRY I DID
NOT GET A CHANCE TO
MEET YOU IN PERSON...
    Good Luck
    Charles Mingus

CHAPTER 14

California Dreamin' with Cass Elliot

1969: Neil Armstrong, commander of Apollo 11, becomes the first man to walk on the moon.

"Cass had prepared for Las Vegas by spending three weeks in bed with nervous flutters, punctuated by attacks of nausea and stomach cramps. While Cass was dealing with her vapors, a show had been put together. Harvey Brooks, a highly talented bass player from the defunct Electric Flag, had assembled a six-man rock band to back Cass. To back the rock band, a 20-piece house orchestra was added in Las Vegas."

—William Kloman, *Esquire*, June 1969

I first met Mama Cass Elliot when Mike Bloomfield invited her to sing backup on The Electric Flag's first single, "Groovin' is Easy," for Columbia Records. Both Buddy and Mike were trying to get Cass to join the band, and while she loved the Flag, she was thinking that her next move would be to launch her own solo career.

After the session, Cass wanted to talk. Leaving her entourage behind, we took off in Cass' orange-mustard-colored Aston Martin to Canter's Deli, since we were both foodie Jews from New York. Cass ordered a turkey Reuben and I ordered a corned beef on rye with chicken soup. Cass was becoming increasingly unhappy with The Mamas and the Papas, especially the continuing stream of personal insults by John Phillips over her weight and other band issues. This was the major factor that was pushing her to go out on her own.

After about two hours of venting to me, a hometown stranger, we went our separate ways and I did not see her again during the Flag sessions. I had come into Cass Elliot's life at a pivotal time in her career. She had become famous with The Mamas and the Papas after their mega hit, "Monday, Monday." Though the sound of the group was based on vocal harmonies arranged by the songwriter, John Phillips, who was also the group's leader, it was Cass' voice that was essential to the group's overall sound.

About a year later, my friend, producer John Simon, was hired by Cass to produce her first solo album, *Dream a Little Dream*. John hired me to play bass on the album since we were all already connected and comfortable working together. We recorded the album in 10 days at Wally Heider Studios in Los Angeles, a major recording facility at that time. My buddy, Paul Harris, played organ and piano; Brenda Holloway did the back-up vocals; Plas Johnson played saxophone; John Sebastian played guitar and harmonica; Stephen Stills was on guitar; Jim Gordon played drums; and Elvis veteran James Burton was on guitar, dobro and banjo.

Burton and I sat next to each other in the studio. I noticed he had the banjo and asked him about it. He said, "I'll tell you a secret. I tune it like a guitar using banjo strings." The album was released in 1968 and had very positive reviews.

The title song, "Dream a Little Dream," was produced by Lou

Adler and was recorded before I was hired for the sessions. Joe Osborn played bass on it. This recording allowed Cass to open up and expand her personal choices beyond The Mamas and the Papas.

Dream a Little Dream, the album, contains touches of country, blues, rock, jazz, gospel and bluegrass. Dunhill Records, who had The Mamas and the Papas under contract and extended it to Cass' solo work, didn't approve of what today is a classic album. They thought it branched out too far.

Shortly after *Dream a Little Dream*, Cass called to see if I might be interested in putting a band together for her upcoming show at Caesars Palace, Las Vegas in October. At that time, I was staying in Los Angeles at the Chateau Marmont working on a few new projects. The Chateau had quite a reputation with many notorious musicians and actors like Jim Morrison and John Belushi, who died of a drug overdose there in Bungalow 3.

Cass suggested that I move into her house in Laurel Canyon so that I could be on call 24/7 to prepare for her show. This way I would be close by and easily available to talk about the songs and arrangements. A few days later, I left the Chateau Marmont and drove up Mulholland Drive in my VW camper to Cass' wood-frame and stone two-story house.

The house was surrounded by an overgrown Victorian Rose garden on several acres of land. Her Aston Martin sports car was sitting in the carport. The toys of Cass' daughter, Owen Vanessa, about two years old at the time, were scattered across the front yard. Several caretakers were always present at her residence.

A swimming pool was in the back of the house and Cass' kitchen was always stocked with gourmet food delivered regularly from the best stores in Beverly Hills. The house was furnished with comfortable sofas and chairs, lots of lamps and high-quality audio equipment. Posters and paintings decorated her walls. My room was on the second floor, one of five bedrooms in the house.

Living at Cass' house was like living in a pop music fish bowl. Los Angeles music royalty was constantly stopping by. Because of Cass' good nature and friendliness, the house became a magnet for musicians. David Crosby was a frequent guest, since he liked to swim. So was John Sebastian, Graham Nash, Stephen Stills and Joni Mitchell. Charles Manson, soon to be the convicted murderer at the Sharon Tate home down the road, visited her refrigerator, though I never saw him.

Cass told me that she wanted to have a band that would kick ass. I began to take notes while sitting in the living room in the early evenings. This Vegas show was her first solo live performance since leaving The Mamas and the Papas and she told me she was nervous and wanted to be at her best. She was comfortable enough with me to share that her so-called friends and enemies would be there watching and waiting for her to fail.

To prepare, she had started dieting. I could not help but notice that Cass was not well. While she was dieting for the show to achieve a "new look" (she lost 100 of 300 pounds), she was also getting stoned more frequently. A couple of her boyfriends, who always seemed to be at the house, made sure of this.

One was Pic Dawson, who got Cass hooked on heroin. Though I never witnessed it, he and Cass would go into her bedroom to drink heroin cocktails. I was savvy enough to know what was going on. Though she did the heroin privately, I knew it was slowly killing her. Her other boyfriend, Billy Doyle, supplied Cass with Iranian hashish. The hashish was laid out on a coffee table for everyone to enjoy. Cass' voice was now shot and was getting worse with each passing day.

We began to develop a routine. We would get together in the late afternoons, talk about the songs and the show. I had brought in New

York session guitarist Hugh McCracken; my old friend Paul Harris; Skip Prokop from the Canadian band, The Paupers, to play drums; and percussionist, Reinol Andino. Jimmy Haskel did the arrangements for the Caesars Palace orchestra. We had two sets of background singers — both male and female. It was quickly becoming a nightmare extravaganza.

The kind of show Cass wanted was dependent on her standing up as a driving force that could front the band through the show. But she wouldn't rehearse, and it was becoming a problem. I'd speak with Cass the night before scheduled rehearsals and she'd promise to be there. "It's gonna be great. We'll talk in the morning," she'd say. And then she wouldn't show. This happened day after day. Shows in Las Vegas are usually highly rehearsed. Even old pros like Frank Sinatra leave no detail untouched.

Cass just brushed off the rehearsal process, saying everything would be fine. At the same time, she continued to lose weight and overmedicate. Without rehearsals, we had a recipe for disaster. I would sit with her, trying to build up her confidence while trying to get her onto some sort of rehearsal schedule. She was enthusiastic when we talked, but I could hear how her voice was deteriorating. This went on for three weeks and it was not getting better.

One afternoon, while floating in Cass' pool, smoking some reefer, I was joined by Stephen Stills and Graham Nash. While we were casually floating and smoking, they told me about this band they were putting together and asked if I would like to play bass. Paul Harris was already in to play keyboards and Dallas Taylor was to be the drummer. Stills and I had played together on *Super Session*, so we knew it would be a comfortable fit.

The band would eventually become Crosby, Stills and Nash. Ironically, the group sang together for the first time at Cass' insistence, who noted that their voices blended well together. In later years, they dedicated an album to her for her early encouragement.

As the Caesars Palace show approached, I went to buy three stylish custom suits at Barry Certo Custom Tailors on Sunset Boulevard. Each suit in 1968 dollars cost $1,000. After spending three hours picking materials and styles, they told me that only one would be ready for me before the show. The other two, they promised, would be delivered to Caesars Palace the day after the opening. I had to pay for all three suits up front — $3,000 plus tax and delivery charges.

As I stepped out of Certo's, a hazy, smog-weighted rain hit the streets like slimy, slippery syrup. Suddenly, out of the corner of my eye, I could see a red Chevy Impala convertible sliding in slow motion with brakes applied into a Lincoln Continental making an illegal left turn onto Sunset Boulevard. I couldn't help but think this was a harbinger of what was about to occur in the coming days in Las Vegas.

We arrived at Caesars Palace on October 5, the Saturday before our Monday night opening. We checked into the Roman-inspired, 700-room casino hotel. After check-in, I called a band meeting to hand out charts. I then dropped off Jimmie Haskell's charts for the 20-piece house orchestra. Before long, it was time for the run through and dress rehearsal in the Circus Maximus, the hotel's 950-seat main showroom.

Over the years, the top entertainers of the world had performed on this stage. Frank Sinatra, Judy Garland, Liberace, Cher, Johnny Mathis, Diana Ross, Bette Midler, Tom Jones, Peggy Lee, Tony Bennett and Sammy Davis Jr. had played the legendary venue. Now, Cass Elliot was to be added to this star-studded list.

At our first rehearsal, Cass walked up to the microphone, looked around and tried to sing a few notes. Nothing came out — she couldn't sing — not even a note. The nightmare I had been having for weeks was now in my face! A sense of dread permeated every member of the band as we watched the scene unfold.

I tried to talk to Cass about her options. Herbal teas, easier tunes, shorter set lists — but she would not hear me. Cass took off to her room, but not without stopping at the Noshorium, the hotel coffee shop. There, she signed autographs and joked with the waitresses like nothing was wrong. On Sunday, her voice was still shot and Cass did not rehearse at all.

A full rehearsal was set on the Circus stage for Monday afternoon. As the house staff prepared the room for the dinner show, my small six-member band plus the 20-member house orchestra arrived. Cass had an old honky-tonk piano — shipped in at great expense — to add an old-time sound to one song. At the rehearsal, she worked out a few numbers and threw out her expensive pre-written script. "Honesty is all you need," she confidently told the skeptical band members.

Just hours before curtain, Cass was running a fever. She told friends her vocal cords were hemorrhaging. If common sense had prevailed, Bobby Roberts, Cass' manager and co-founder of Dunhill Records, would have cancelled this show. All of us close to Cass urged him to do this. He said, "It is too late and she will just have to get through it." In my opinion, Roberts hung Cass out to dry.

Backstage, flowers were arriving. One arrangement came from Joan Baez, who was in Nashville making an album, and another arrived from Mia Farrow, who was in New Orleans. In the meantime, Cass was drinking hot tea with lemon. When told by her secretary, Carol Samuels, that John and Michelle were at the hotel, Cass said, "Screw 'em!"

The Monday night opening drew a very high-profile crowd. Jimi Hendrix was there. Vegas royalty, Peter Lawford and Sammy Davis Jr. came. Cass was picking up the tab for all of them — about 200 friends, guests and press members in the front of the house.

Meanwhile, Dawson and Doyle were backstage getting Cass high. She smoked hashish and later admitted she had taken heroin as well before going on stage. Now, she was not only sick, but stoned as well. By the time she went on stage, Cass was nearly in a comatose state. There was little doubt now that short of cancelling the show, this was a disaster in the making.

The show began badly. I counted off and the orchestra started playing her overture. Cass mistook the music for a cue and started singing "California Earthquake" over a backstage microphone. The mic was quickly killed.

There was some scattered applause as the curtain opened to reveal our group. Cass' hair looked disheveled and her timing was way off. She sang a half a tone flat on every number. She forgot the names of songs and began to express her disenchantment with The Mamas and the Papas, apparently forgetting the group's members were sitting in the front of the audience. She even told the audience she hated the group's music and being under John's thumb.

This angered many in the unsympathetic audience, who wanted to hear the group's music, not Cass' choices. As the show went on, she continued to miss cues and flub lines. The audience turned on her and many began to noisily walk out.

Conversation among the band members had been kept to a minimum. We were all trying to stay professional, but we all felt empathy for her in this disastrous situation. It was hard as a friend, which I had become, to watch her go down this way. At the end, there was no applause for an encore. Cass returned to the stage and apologized to the audience for her mistakes. And then she closed with "Dream a Little Dream." Unfortunately, it wasn't over. There was to be a second show that night.

As Cass came offstage, she got another piece of unsettling news. The marquee in the front of the hotel, which had initially said Cass

Elliot, had been changed to "Mama" Cass Elliot, which she hated, since it put her back into The Mamas and the Papas. The slight was another nail in her professional coffin. The second show was equally bad, if not worse. The entire night was a total disaster.

Newsweek compared the performance to the Titanic, writing that "Like some great ocean liner embarking on an ill-fated maiden voyage, Mama Cass slid down the waves and sank to the bottom." Other reviews were equally devastating.

During the night, without consulting Cass, Caesars Palace and Bobby Roberts came to an agreement to end what was to have been a lucrative $40,000 a week engagement. Roberts never informed me that the show had been cancelled. I learned of it the next day on a morning walk outside Caesars Palace, when I looked up and saw that Cass' name had been removed from the marquee and replaced by another performer.

Cass immediately flew home, where she was admitted into a hospital and had her tonsils removed. She was more than $90,000 in debt, owing money for virtually every part of the show from the musicians to the lighting technicians to a $10,000 script that was never used.

I called Roberts in an attempt to get paid, but he would not take my call. We the musicians never saw a dime from that gig. My guys had their plane tickets and were very understanding as only friends can be. And my two suits from Certo's that I had bought and paid for never showed up!

I had to go back to Los Angeles to Cass' house to get my things. I did not see her there and never heard from Cass Elliot again.

CHAPTER 15

New Doors Opening

1970: Four students at Kent State University in Ohio are slain by National Guardsmen at a demonstration protesting the U.S. incursion into Cambodia.

I think part of the reason memories of life at Cass' house remain so vague to me is because I purposely avoided much of the insanity of her lifestyle. Yes, I smoked some hash, ate the great catered food and lounged by the pool, as the other visitors did, but I always viewed myself as outside of her crowd. I consciously avoided the intense drug use and the self-indulgent hangers-on that surrounded her there.

After Cass' disastrous performance in Vegas, I was in a funk. My name was attached to the fiasco and I could not pay my musicians. I was scheduled to be in New York to begin rehearsals with Crosby, Stills and Nash. Before heading back to my home in Mill Valley, I stopped off to visit with my friends, John Sebastian and John Simon, at a counterculture community called The Farm.

The Farm was in Los Angeles on Barham Boulevard, near the Warner Brothers Studios in Burbank. This Farm, once a hunting lodge, was home to many musicians, artists, actors and photographers. It also included the Firesign Theatre and Tie-Dye Annie, whose real name was Ann Thomas, a former copywriter for Capitol Records. She was noted for perfecting the art form of tie-dying, which she had taught to John Sebastian, who had taken up residency there while he was working on his album, *John B. Sebastian.*

John Simon also hung out at The Farm while producing Cass Elliott's album, *Dream a Little Dream.* While there, Simon hooked up with a resident who later became his wife. He was planning to take her back to see his East Coast neighborhood and offered to drive my 1963 Volkswagen camper across the country and deliver it to me in Sag Harbor. This arrangement freed me to take care of some loose ends before leaving the west coast to go back east.

I flew home to Mill Valley to pack and clean out my house, which I gave to Mike Bloomfield. With that finished, my days in Mill Valley were over. The Electric Flag was history and I took off for the next phase of my life. My airline tickets from California with expenses were covered by Crosby, Stills and Nash.

I was still only 25 years old and not very savvy about business. To me, everything was about the music that I loved to play. I have always had a very simple view of the world. So, with only a verbal agreement — nothing in writing from Crosby, Stills and Nash — I took my seat on the plane and headed for the east coast. I would soon learn that the devil is in the details. What's left unsaid and unwritten usually comes back to haunt you!

Once in Sag Harbor, Paul Harris and I moved in with John Sebastian. It was John who had encouraged David Crosby, Stephen Stills and Graham Nash to get out of Los Angeles to rehearse and to avoid the constant compliments from all the "yes men" in the area. When Paul and I arrived, it was the middle of the winter. John's house was covered with snow and looked like a scenic Hallmark greeting card. Paul and I were fighting jet lag. The freezing weather was a shock to our California systems, even though Paul and I are both native New Yorkers.

In a short time, we started rehearsals with Crosby, Stills and Nash at Stills' nearby house. From the very beginning, the musical chemistry wasn't right between us. I had come to Sag Harbor to be a creative bass player — my specialty as a musician.

But Stephen Stills wanted someone to follow his instructions precisely and play the basslines that he specified. We were immediately on totally different tracks.

John Sebastian was also at the rehearsals and sometimes found himself tapping along on a drum kit in the room. In an interview for this book, Sebastian recalled that Stills suddenly stopped and said, "You know...this is exactly what we need. I don't know why we are looking for bad-ass drummers. This is going to be an acoustic guitar thing. We need a guy who can just keep the time and bump along with us. You'd be another voice and another songwriter. Who knows?"

Sebastian said he turned the group down, since he had decided his future was to become a solo artist. "I wasn't sure I could make the transition back to band life," he said. "At that point, those guys were very much in love — if I can use the term loosely. That was a very tight unit. I didn't feel like I was in as deep as these guys were."

When we were all in LA, I was told that I would be an equal group member. However, when I got to Sag Harbor, the principal members of the band saw me as a sideman only. Getting paid as a sideman does not cover the expenses, even with per diem, of your home and on the road life, since you are living the same life style as the principals but you are being paid as a replaceable sideman with no opportunities to participate in the royalty pool. From day one, I was unhappy with my situation. It was a brutal lesson to learn. I wanted to contribute my musical ideas but had the door shut. We were incompatible. The same thing was happening to keyboard player Paul Harris. We had a band meeting to clear the air.

Crosby later said in an interview that Stills felt I was too good a bass player. Translated, that means I was an independent thinker, which is not what the group wanted. They wanted a bass player who would do as he was told. This was not what they had offered me in the pool at Cass' house.

Interestingly, in the music business, one is rarely outright fired. Just as I learned of the cancellation of Cass' show in Las Vegas from an outdoor billboard, it would happen a similar way with Crosby, Stills and Nash. After our business discussion, the band quit talking to Paul and myself. There was just dead silence. Always a bad sign.

The band was scheduled to do some out-of-town recording and we didn't know whether we were part of it or not. Finally, I called the band's manager, David Geffen, about plane tickets for these sessions. Geffen didn't take the call, but his secretary told me there were no tickets for Paul or myself. That's how we learned that our services were no longer needed.

On a lighter note, I would not speak with Stephen Stills again until 2004, when my wife, Bonnie, answered his call on the phone at 3 a.m. at our home in Tucson, Arizona. At first, I thought it was a prank call, so I asked him some personal history questions that he and I had shared. It was Stephen all right. He was coming to Tucson and wanted me to play bass on a blues album he was recording. We then started negotiating my fee. Believe it or not, it took over an hour! When we finally came to an agreement, I hung up the phone, looked over at Bonnie and said, "That session will never happen." I was right, it didn't.

When one door closes, another always opens. John Sebastian was getting ready to finish his *John B. Sebastian* album that he started in Los Angeles and asked Paul, Dallas and myself to record with him. Sitting in John's backyard rehearsal studio waiting for John on day one of a four-day rehearsal, we discussed life after these sessions. Paul was going home to his loft in Soho with wife Susie Campbell to do sessions and gigs in Manhattan. Dallas decided he was going to stay with Crosby, Stills and Nash because it was a guaranteed paycheck and the music was more important than the money.

We rehearsed for four or five days at John's home studio and then all travelled to Manhattan to Jerry Ragovoy's Hit Factory to complete the project. My friend, Paul Rothchild, was the producer.

The sessions with Sebastian were great. John was going though personal problems with his marriage, but you would never know it. His sessions were musical, fun and soulful. Rothchild being the great producer that he was, kept the sessions flowing and the tunes tight. I played on three tunes. "Red-Eye Express," "Baby Don't You Get Crazy" and "Fa-Fana-Fa."

The album's release was marred by legal controversy, with two record companies, Reprise and MGM, claiming ownership of the recording and simultaneously distributing the album for several months in 1970. Reprise, with whom John had signed as a solo artist in 1969, ultimately sued MGM, Sebastian's former distributor, for copyright infringement to settle the dispute, with the MGM release of the album subsequently withdrawn from the market. *John B. Sebastian* is one of John's most successful solo albums.

After the sessions were completed, back in Sag Harbor, I rented the downstairs of an old farmhouse on the Main Street leading into the downtown. I was living alone with my instant home kit consisting of a red and black oriental-patterned nine-by-twelve foot rug, floor pillow, wooden stool, typewriter, portable stereo, two-track tape recorder, albums, tapes and cardboard file cabinet filled with poems, lyrics, lead sheets and business stuff. I stayed in the farmhouse for six months. This was a period of solitude and self-examination. No gigs, no sessions.

Finally, in the spring of 1970, I left Sag Harbor and went into Manhattan to set up camp with Paul and Susie Harris, who had a loft on 112 Greene Street in the West Village (now SoHo).

Janis Joplin

While I was there, I got a call from Albert Grossman's office saying that Albert and Janis Joplin were at the Bitter End and they wanted me to join them there for drinks. I quickly put myself together and took off for the club. Albert and Janis were at a back corner table schmoozing with Paul Colby, owner of the Bitter End.

I first met Janis Joplin at a party at her house in San Francisco. Nick Gravenites drove me over to meet her. Janis was a new experience for me. Most women I was acquainted with were feminine and smelled nice. Janis smelled of patchouli oil, Southern Comfort and sweat. I met Nick's ex-wife Linda there, who I believe was Janis' girl friend though I wouldn't swear to it, and somebody else who was her boyfriend. Nick introduced me and then walked away. As soon as he was gone Janis asked if I liked Nick's singing, laughed and took off across the room. I started to follow but suddenly she was in the arms of someone she seemed to know better than me. I never got to know her well.

When I sat down at the table the conversation was in full swing about Janis doing a special show with a band that they thought I would put together for the Bitter End. The tequila and Southern Comfort continued to flow and the conversation was ongoing between Janis thinking about tunes she could do, Albert with little cutting remarks and Paul Colby creating an ad campaign for a spontaneous Janis Jam show with me suggesting players. After several hours of banter, the curtain fell with the conclusion by Janis that this project might upset existing members of her band. Janis wanted to go someplace else and do something or someone.

At that point, me, Janis and her associates, I never did get their names, went across the street for a nightcap at the Cafe Au Go Go. There, we ran into Jim Morrison and his bodyguard, Tony. Jim was fired up and ready to go...anywhere. By this time, the alcohol consumption level was pretty high. I offered up the loft of my good friend, Paul Harris, where I was camping out. It was just a couple of blocks away and was already set up to jam. Paul called in drummer Wells Kelly who was staying at Jim Tunicks loft on the fifth floor and was set up and ready to play by the time we walked across Houston Street to the loft at 112 Greene Street.

Paul's loft was on the first floor, making an easy entrance for our highly intoxicated group. After an hour of more drinking, Janis was now in the mood to start singing Sam & Dave's "Hold On, I'm Coming." Paul, Wells and I did our imitation of Booker T. & the MG's with Jim Morrison trying the harmony part. He then quickly launched into his unique howling. By the end of the song, Jim was down on his knees out of control with Janis laughing and pouring her glass of Jose Cuervo over his head. Then they launched into a slow blues tune about the human condition that both Janis and Jim sang spontaneously.

We continued our crawl up to Steve Paul's The Scene club on West 46th Street in the theatre district. There we added Tiny Tim to our mix, an anomaly sitting at a back table smirking and making funny noises with his ukulele. Guitarist Rick Derringer had the house band at The Scene. Jimi Hendrix came in to jam with Buddy Miles. While setting up, Hendrix and Miles eyed Morrison and myself and called us up to join the mix. Morrison was still howling as I played. Somewhere out there is a bootleg recording of this very creative performance.

Janis was one of the stars of the Haight Ashbury community. I caught her performance at the Avalon Ballroom with the Grateful Dead when I first arrived in San Francisco. She patterned herself after the true black blues heroines like Bessie Smith and Ma Rainey. Not your usual Texas woman, Janis was outspoken and dared to be different. She didn't have a great voice or the best vocal licks, but she reached into your soul to make her mark.

The Monterey Pop Festival was her breakthrough performance. Big Brother played on Saturday and Sunday. Janis was dressed in her historic costume designed by Linda Gravenites. In D.A. Pennebaker's documentary *Monterey Pop*, you can see a few cutaway shots of the audience with Cass Elliot watching Janis perform "Ball and Chain" with Big Brother. A picture of amazement and awe was on her face.

Pennebaker had to discreetly film the performance on Saturday and Sunday since he was told that he could not film Janis and her band on orders from their manager, Julius Karpen. The band members did battle with Karpen and he was overruled.

Backstage the band met with Albert Grossman, who they signed with several months later after Karpen was fired. Big Brother and the Holding Company stayed a California band even after they signed with Grossman in New York. Their first tour on the East Coast started in Philadelphia followed by a gig in New York City at the Anderson Theatre. The last day of their tour in April 1968, the band headlined with Jimi Hendrix, Buddy Guy, Joni Mitchell, Richie Havens, Paul Butterfield and Elvin Bishop at the wake and concert for Rev. Martin Luther King Jr.

"Joplin was the most staggering leading woman in rock...she slinks like tar, scowls like war ... clutching the knees in her final stanza, begging it not to leave. Janis Joplin can sing the chic off any listener," wrote Richard Goldstein in the May 1968 issue of *Vogue* magazine. Her persona included profanities, jokes, drinking Southern Comfort, outspoken sexuality and love of life.

My mentor and friend, John Simon, produced Joplin's *Cheap Thrills*, which he did while we both were working on the second Electric Flag album *An American Music Band* and Cass Elliot's

Dream a Little Dream.

The album cover design was by underground cartoonist Robert Crumb. The record hit #1 on the Billboard 200 albums chart eight weeks after its release and sold over a million copies.

Buying My First Apartment

In the same 112 Greene Street building where Paul Harris lived, there was a loft owned by Jim Tunick, a then music producer/entrepreneur. Jim had created a jam space where musicians could meet other musicians and try out their songs. Paul had introduced us and brought me up there to play one evening. When Jim opted to move to the East Village, he offered to sell the loft to me. I jumped at the deal, since I was ready to buy my first place. It was 1969 in the West Village. That loft cost me all of $5,000!

When I took ownership, the place required a lot of work. The wood floors needed to be replaced, the toilet was exposed and there was no sink, shower or walls. One of my neighbors, an artistic carpenter, offered to work with me. He shared his expertise, teaching me how to curve plywood, the technique I used to build my circular bathroom. Together we built room dividers, bookcases and a small performance stage. This work kept me busy for about six months.

Shortly after I moved in, I got a call from Eric Clapton saying that he was in town with Bonnie & Delaney and all of them wanted to come over. Carl Radle, their bass player, wanted to meet me, as well as the rest of the band. They were also looking for a place to hang out and listen to and share some music. At that time, the loft had only a couch and some chairs and an exposed toilet on a platform directly behind the couch. Bonnie asked me where the john was, and I pointed to the solitary toilet. I said, "Nobody look" and off she went. A real trouper!

After the disaster in Las Vegas with Cass Elliot and then getting fired by Crosby, Stills and Nash, I was depressed. I was doing scattered sessions but didn't want to be around people who would ask me how I was doing or what I was up to. I realized that sometimes a person succeeds and sometimes they don't. Both, however, require the same amount of effort.

Then, out of the blue, the phone rang. On the line was Jack Gold, vice president at Columbia Records, offering me a staff producer job. I told him I'd think about it. But by the end of our conversation, he had made me an offer I could not refuse. I took the job immediately.

Then, I reflected on the last six months of my life and turned a page!

CHAPTER 16

The Miles Davis Experience

1971: Jim Morrison, lead singer of The Doors, dies in Paris at age 27.

A week after getting the call from Jack Gold, I found myself employed at Columbia Records with an office, a desk and a secretary named Mary. It was my first paying day job in the music business. The title on my business card was impressive: Staff Producer!

My job was to scout for new rock, blues and psychedelic groups, areas where Columbia was behind the times. The label encouraged me to take my time, look for talent and then produce the demos of possible new talent and groups. My first find was John Hall who eventually became the leader of pop band "Orleans" who had chart hits with "Dance with Me" and "Still the One". I met John at a jam session and was impressed with his guitar playing and songwriting.

On November 7, 2006, Hall was elected as a Democrat to the United States House of Representatives from the state of New York. He served in congress until 2011.

Once a week, all producers would meet with Clive Davis, then president of Columbia Records, to pitch our demos. If our ideas made it past the meeting, we had a green light to go forward with a budget. I played the John Hall demo for Clive who gave me the go ahead.

The next demo I played for Clive that he approved was a great R&B singer name Bobby Lester who was working at a nine to five job in Queens. We did a single with Bobby called "Sweet Gentle Nighttime" which Clive loved. To paraphrase Clive, some do and some don't. Unfortunately for all concerned this was a *don't*.

My office was the first one in view as a visitor passed the reception desk. There were four to five offices on each side of a long narrow corridor as you looked down to the left. The office next to mine was occupied by Teo Macero, Miles Davis' producer.

Before starting at Columbia, I didn't know Macero personally, only by reputation. He was a legendary producer, jazz saxophonist and composer. At Columbia over 20 years, Macero had produced hundreds of records, including Miles' epic, *Kind of Blue*. He had also worked with Charles Mingus, Duke Ellington, Ella Fitzgerald, Thelonious Monk, Johnny Mathis, Count Basie, Dave Brubeck, Tony Bennett, Charlie Byrd and Stan Getz.

I was sitting in my office on a Monday getting my week together when I received a call on my office intercom from Teo Macero, inviting me to join him for a cup of coffee in his office. We settled into a conversation with Teo casually sharing that Miles would be doing a demo for his wife, Betty, who was an R&B artist. He said "Miles wants to use an electric bass. Would you be interested in playing on the demo?" My answer was "Sure, I'd love to"....thinking to myself, Are are you fuckin' kidding? I was being offered a chance to play with the great Miles Davis. I had to pinch myself.

The session was in May 1969 at Columbia's Studios on 49 East 52nd Street in Manhattan. As I walked through the control room into the studio, I bumped into Miles going out as I was coming in. He looked at me, cocked his head to the right and said, "Fat, white muthafucker, what are you doin' here?"

At this stage, I hadn't personally experienced the Miles Davis acerbic sense of humor. He jabbed a left to my right arm and said, "Just fuckin' with you."

167

I would soon learn that Miles was like that. He was the kind of guy who, once he found one of your buttons, wouldn't really push it hard, but would push the edges a bit just to make you nervous. It wasn't malicious, but it was testy. His values were specific, and he wanted everything and everyone to relate to those values.

If he had to shake you up a bit, then that's what he would do to get control of the moment. He valued controlled chaos and liked to keep everyone around him off balance.

Betty, who was only 23 at the time, had met Miles in 1967 and they were married a year later. She had a strong influence on him, from the latest fashion to new music. She had recently introduced Miles to Jimi Hendrix and Sly Stone, rock innovators that Miles would borrow from. This would become apparent on his next album.

In addition to my electric bass, the band for the demo was made up of drummer Mitch Mitchell from Jimi Hendrix's band, John McLaughlin on guitar, Joe Zawinul and Herbie Hancock on electric piano and Larry Young on the Hammond B3 organ. I had not met any of these excellent musicians before except for Mitch but had heard their recorded work and was a little nervous. I had met Mitch at Monterey Pop Festival.

Every time I heard Miles in the headsets — saying "try this" or suggesting where to come in — I was in awe. But I also realized he was just a guy trying to make things happen. I caught a buzz taking direction from a master musician that I'd been listening to for years and had the utmost respect for.

Betty Davis is a beautiful woman and knows how to hold the attention of an audience. In my opinion, she was too funky for Columbia Records at that time. Jazz was one thing, but nasty, sexy R&B was not the label's strong point in 1969. So, after the demo, they passed on signing her. Mike Lang who signed my later band, The Fabulous Rhinestones, eventually enlisted her for his Just Sunshine

Records label.

Miles and I had some sporadic conversations in the studio during Betty's session. He told me Jack DeJohnette, his drummer, turned him onto my bass playing on an Eric Mercury record, *Electric Black Man*.

"I thought you were great on that," he told me. After the session was over and I was packing up to leave, Miles came over to me and said "Hey, Haaavey. I'm doing some sessions, check with Teo for the schedule."

Now, hip to Miles' sense of humor and past the "respectful" stage of our relationship, I sarcastically responded, "I'll see if I can fit you in." He said, "heh." Of course, to have this opportunity to add my music to the mix Miles was creating was truly an honor for me.

Perhaps the most important thing to come out of Betty's demo was Miles' newfound and growing appreciation for the sound of the electric bass. I didn't know it at the time, but Miles, through his friendships with my old friend, Jimi, and Sly Stone, was becoming increasingly enamored with not only electric instruments, but the blues.

The blues was not at all new to Miles. When he visited Chicago, Miles would go to a club on Monday nights to hear Muddy Waters perform. "I knew I had to get some of what he was doing up there in my music," Miles wrote in his biography. "You know, the sound of the $1.50 drums and the harmonicas and the two-chord blues." Miles liked what Jimi, as well as James Brown, were doing and appreciated their grounding in the blues.

By 1969, Miles was ready for another major change in his music. His 1960's quintet, with Tony Williams on drums, Herbie Hancock on keyboards, Ron Carter on upright bass and Wayne Shorter on sax, had been together for five years. Though the band was one of the greats, for Miles, the sound was getting tired. He was restless for his next new thing.

Gregory Davis, Miles' son — in an interview for this book — said his father didn't change his musical direction simply for the sake of change. "The music wanted to change," he said. "His creativity told him a sound wouldn't be in style much longer. This is what you need to do. He just inherently knew that. It was the music that told him to change."

Miles' previous album, *In a Silent Way*, released July 30 1969, reflected his initial interest in electric music. It also signaled Miles' stylistic shift to jazz fusion and featured virtuoso electric guitarist and newcomer John McLaughlin, who Miles first heard only the night before the recording session. The pianos used on the album were electric, but the other instruments were acoustic. David Holland, the amazingly talented bass player for Miles, played upright bass on *In a Silent Way*.

The next album, which would become *Bitches Brew*, would get Miles' first full-blown electric treatment. It would signal a new direction for Miles' music and I found myself a part of it — though I was clueless exactly how I would fit.

The night before the studio session in August 1969, for what would become *Bitches Brew*, I was called for a rehearsal at Miles' two-story apartment at 312 77th Street in New York City. The living room had four or five tiers — all filled with musicians led by Joe Zawinul sitting at the Fender Rhodes piano at floor level facing the band. Little did I know it at the time, but history was being made that night.

Zawinul contributed the 20-minute track, "Pharaoh's Dance," which would occupy the whole of side one of the landmark album we were beginning to rehearse. From this, he would go on to become one of the creators of jazz fusion, an innovative musical genre that combined jazz with elements of rock and world music. Later,

Zawinul co-founded the groups Weather Report and the globally oriented Zawinul Syndicate.

None of us knew how long the rehearsal would last that night. Miles was relaxed, casual and just kind of hanging out. I got the feeling at the time I was in a musical chemistry experiment. It turns out that feeling was correct, but the direction, as most things with Miles Davis, would surprise me.

There was a small bass amp sitting on the second tier level, so I plugged in, sat down and made myself comfortable. I looked around for Dave Holland, the regular bass player, but he wasn't there. I had long admired him and was looking forward to our first meeting.

Joe Zawinul began playing a theme, which we all picked up on and played for awhile. Suddenly, Miles cut the band. He had something to show us. Out came some Jack Johnson boxing film reels, which he then proceeded to thread into a projector. The film played for the next hour or so.

Jack Johnson, who died in 1946, was a Texas-born boxer nicknamed the "Galveston Giant." At the height of the Jim Crow era, he became the first African-American world heavyweight boxing champion. He faced much controversy when he was charged with violating the Mann Act in 1912 (an anti-prostitution law), even though there was an obvious lack of evidence and the charge was largely racially based. For more than a decade, Johnson was the most famous and the most notorious African-American on the planet. In 2018 — 72 years after his death — Johnson received a presidential pardon.

Miles revered Johnson because he was not only a great boxer, but a black hero. He would mimic some of Johnson's graceful reflexes, not making many comments. Johnson was inspirational and had great moves. But you intuitively knew why he was watching it. Miles was into the moves. Those boxing moves inspired him in the making of *Bitches Brew*. He would later make similar moves when we were recording. He had a controlled rhythm when we were in the studio.

Gregory Davis, Miles' son, told Frank Beacham he knew the film well, since his father projected it for him while teaching him to box as a kid. It also didn't hurt that Johnson liked jazz and often played upright bass at his own nightclub in Texas.

"My father tried to pattern Jack's rhythm from those boxing moves…he'd use it as part of his personal style and to keep himself in shape. When you are playing that horn, you have to stay in shape."

Miles was close friends with Sugar Ray Robinson, the boxing champion, who helped train him at Harry Wiley's Gym at Broadway and 136th Street in New York City. Wiley was Robinson's trainer and Gregory trained there as well with his father.

Gregory said he was 12 years old when introduced to boxing by his father. "My father pushed me into boxing because he loved it. When I got into boxing seriously, I won my little smokers — I won them all. But my father couldn't deal with the fact that I might get hurt. He couldn't sit there and see me in a combative situation."

As he grew up, Gregory said he "became the most successful member of his Army boxing team while he was stationed in Germany during the Vietnam war." He won several awards, to the great pride of his father. In later years, they lived and traveled together.

Paul Johnson, a Harlem resident who also trained at the gym, told the New York Times that Sugar Ray Robinson taught Miles much of what he knew about boxing. "He hurt a few musicians who didn't want to listen," Johnson said of Miles. "He knew how to use his hands. Sugar Ray taught him."

Later, in 1971, Miles would release an album called *A Tribute to Jack Johnson*. It would use many of the same players on *Bitches Brew* and would reflect the deep integration of boxing and music in Miles' work. But on the night of the rehearsal, I had no idea where the Jack Johnson film or any of the boxing lore fit into our work ahead.

I left the rehearsal that night no more informed about what we were actually doing than when I had arrived at the apartment. But I got a great buzz from hanging with Miles and talking with Joe Zawinul. The next day the session began at 10 a.m. in Studio B on the second floor of Columbia studio complex at 49 East 52nd Street. I don't believe that anyone — including Miles or Teo — knew what was going to happen that day.

A long forest green curtain hung from the ceiling to the floor, cutting the studio in half to create a more intimate feeling. Dave Holland and I were set up next to each other. I had an Ampeg B-15 amplifier in a baffled housing as well as a direct audio feed from my bass to the console. John McLaughlin's guitar amp was near the control room window with drums and percussion spread out alongside him. Keyboards were to the right of the entrance to the studio and horns by the curtain.

There was no song list or written music. To my knowledge at the time, we didn't even have songs, much less know how they were to sound. I found out years later that there were tunes that were presented to Miles and there were other rehearsals before I was recruited. But I never heard about them.

Miles had ideas about the rhythms that he wanted and the instrument groupings for coloring effects that would inspire us. It would be all spontaneous — with each musician entering into a musical improvisational "conversation."

Miles might offer a tempo count, suggest a few chords or give a hint of melody, mood or tone. But that would be about all. He liked to work this way because he thought it forced musicians to pay close attention to one another. On the quieter moments of the recording of *Bitches Brew*, Miles' voice is barely audible. He gives instructions to the musicians or snaps his fingers to indicate tempo. He softly utters "keep it tight" or calls for a solo. Despite his reputation as a cool improviser, much of Miles' performance on the album is aggressive and explosive. He plays fast runs and ventures into the upper register of the trumpet.

For me, I just sat back and locked into Miles' directions. He would point, cut off and use hand signals — creating an abstract sound painting with the musicians as his instrument. It was sort of like viewing the boxing film the night before.

Miles wanted the electric bass to set up a pulsing groove on the bottom. He said, "Just make it feel good." Each take was a performance. Listen, react and respond. I had no idea what any of the music would or should sound like. It seemed like I had stepped onto a rocket ship, blasted off and went into orbit around the planet Miles Davis. The man just let us go. If he wasn't satisfied with what he was getting, he would stop it and move on to something else.

For me, the essential key to the session was listening. Playing with this group of musicians was totally different than any music I was familiar with. It's like that familiar chair you're used to sitting on suddenly gets pulled away and you have to find your balance so you don't fall. It was like being in a conversation when you run out of a word; you bridge it with something to keep the conversation going. Sometimes it's maybe an "ah" or "um," and then you continue speaking. Just this time, we are doing it non-verbally with music.

What I brought to the session more than anything else was a pulse, a bottom. I'm able to get in that bottom and make something happen without jumping around a lot. I think that's what helped the album work. I was just holding the bottom…just punching, kicking but keeping it solid. Dave Holland, on upright bass, was playing melodic fills in-between and around. He has extraordinary chops. I was very in the pocket, a basic kind of guy. Dave has a musical vocabulary that is endless. He is a marvelous musician and it all just spontaneously came together.

When Miles said "OK, this one is a C7 sound" that was the whole chart, which meant to me that C would be the tone center. Miles counts it off and we just started playing. It went that way the entire recording. This was not the way Miles had worked in the past; he was stepping into a new genre. Miles created something new in public. He did it with a big group of musicians in a major studio. It would go out to the world immediately. He created this thing because he could. He had the reputation, the skill and the respect that meant people would automatically listen to it.

After the three-day session ended, it was left to Miles and Teo to make sense of all the recordings. Teo made it work from beginning to end through tape editing and various studio effects. He used tape loops, delays, reverb chambers and echo effects. Through his editing, he concocted many totally new musical structures that were later imitated by the band in live concerts. Teo and Miles created magic with the editing and turned *Bitches Brew* into the major hit that it was.

Released on March 30, 1970, it became Miles' first gold record and sold more than half a million copies. Upon release, it received a mixed response, due to the album's unconventional style and experimental sound. Today, *Bitches Brew* is regarded as one of jazz's greatest albums and a progenitor of the jazz-rock genre, as well as a major influ-  ence on rock and funk musicians. The album won a Grammy Award for "Best Large Jazz Ensemble Album" in 1971.

Son Gregory Davis, who wrote *Dark Magus: The Jekyll and*

Hyde Life of Miles Davis (Backbeat Books, 2006), noted that after *Bitches Brew* his father was very much attracted to electric instruments. "My father felt that electric music in general has more atoms and more sound," he said. "It projected the music. It was not only louder with the amplification, but it offered other enhancements with the gadgets available. You can do things with electricity that you can't do with ordinary acoustic instruments."

Miles Davis would attempt to do an album with Jimi Hendrix and tried to get Paul McCartney to play electric bass on it. Hendrix died before they could play together. Within a couple of years, Miles would meet John Lennon, and in 2006 he was inducted into the Rock & Roll Hall of Fame. Gregory accepted the award on his behalf.

"The boldly experimental soundscapes of Davis' 1969 album, *Bitches Brew*, spoke to the sensibilities of rock fans who'd been digesting the Grateful Dead's expansive improvisations," the Hall of Fame said of Davis' induction. "His forward-thinking sensibility, insatiably curious muse and eagerness to move music into uncharted realms made him a contemporary musician, irrespective of genre."

Electronics also affected Miles Davis' live performances. "He refused to stand in front of microphones anymore," Gregory Davis said. "He wanted electronics in his live performances. He wanted a microphone on his horn and wanted to be able to direct his band from different places on the stage. He was the first horn player that had amplification on his horn. It came about the same time as *Bitches Brew*."

Steve Berkowitz, who is now a producer of Miles Davis archival recordings and a consultant to his estate, called Davis one of the greatest bandleaders who ever lived. "Miles had a genius for picking the right people in his bands," Berkowitz said. "Those players who worked with Miles would play what they play and add to the whole of the music."

"Harvey would look at you and listen to you and then he would play something," Berkowitz continued. "Probably he was making it up, but he seemed to have that on some super level. It would be my guess that not too often did someone tell Harvey what to play. They would ask him to come in and be Harvey Brooks. Harvey could not only listen, but he obviously added his musical contribution.

"It's not that he had a specific style that would make you go 'oh, listen, that's a Harvey Brooks riff.' A James Jamerson or Charles Mingus had a thing, a style. Harvey, on the other hand, had a musical comprehension that was very deep and soulful. I can't describe a style for Harvey. Perhaps the greatest compliment of all is he added to the musical whole of whatever he did."

Also, Berkowitz mentioned that Harvey Brooks and the other musicians at the *Bitches Brew* session were there at the birth of fusion. "Those players were fusing rock, R&B and jazz all together," he said. "That was very important in the development of 20th century American music. Fusion came from the children of Miles."

About two weeks after the sessions ended, I got a call from Miles. He said he needed a name for a track that was going to be on the "B" side of the "Great Expectations" single. He said, "Brooks, give me a name."

I listened to the tune over the phone, which sounded to me like frogs sadly croaking in a pond. I said, "The Little Blue Frog." Miles simply said "Thanks Brooks, later." That's the title that ended up on the record.

Teo told me there would be another session on Jan 28, 1970. I told him I wasn't available because I would be starting work on John Hall's first Columbia album on that same day in San Francisco. When Miles mentioned the possibility of a promotional tour, I told him I would be busy with another project. Truth is I could have moved Hall's album, but I was insecure about my fitting in with

Miles on the road. Sadly, that was our last conversation. I should have taken the gig! Life lesson: Always take the jump forward!

Playing music with Miles and sharing the bass chair with one of my favorite bass players, Dave Holland, was inspiring. Holland, who had only played upright bass prior to *Bitches Brew,* would evolve as well. By the end of 1969, he played electric bass guitar (often using a wah-wah pedal and other electronic effects) with greater frequency as Miles' music became increasingly electronic, amp-based and funky. The influence of Jimi Hendrix was seeping into Miles' musical life. By the end of the summer of 1970, R&B bass guitarist Michael Henderson replaced Holland.

The whole experience with Miles Davis inspired me to replace a lot of useless baggage that had been clogging up my subconscious mind. I look back on my time with him as a defining moment and my entrance into a new world of music.

One final note on my work with Miles. When people see my discography, they note I'm listed as playing on several Miles Davis recordings, including *Big Fun, Miles Davis, Vol 3, Isle of Wight, The Columbia Years 1955-1985, Circle in the Round, Le Meilleur De Miles Davis, The Essential Miles Davis* and *The Best of Miles Davis.* All of the material used on those albums came from our original sessions for *Bitches Brew.* I never recorded with Miles again after that.

CHAPTER 17

From Soho to Woodstock

1972: RCA develops the Compact Disc.

With Miles Davis' album behind me, I settled back into my producing job at Columbia Records. In August 1970 — a year after *Bitches Brew* — I walked past a mix room at Columbia Studios and saw Jimi Hendrix inside working. He waved me in. "Spinning knobs," Jimi said, working in a room that smelled heavily of reefer. He was tweaking some of his recordings.

He was headed back to England, Jimi told me, but when he returned, he wanted me to join him and Miles Davis to discuss working on a new a record project that they were brewing together. It would also include Buddy Miles. I thought the idea was terrific and was excited there was a sliver of hope I would work jointly with both Jimi and Miles again.

Soon after, on August 25, Jimi's own Electric Lady Studios opened for business in Manhattan. A grand opening party was held the next day. Immediately after the party, Jimi left for England. He boarded an Air India flight for London. From there, he went to the Isle of Wight Festival, where he was the headliner. On September 16, Jimi performed in public for the last time during an informal jam at Ronnie Scott's Jazz Club in Soho with Eric Burdon and his band War. Jimi's performance that night was uncharacteristically subdued. He played backing guitar and didn't engage in the typical histrionics he was famous for.

"Jimi spent much of the next day — September 17 — in London with Monika Dannermann at her apartment in the Samarkand Hotel, 22 Lansdowne Cresent, Notting Hill. They spent most of the night talking and finally went to sleep about 7 a.m," a media account said. "At about 11 a.m., Dannermann awoke to find Hendrix breathing, but unconscious and unresponsive. She called an ambulance. Paramedics then transported Jimi to a nearby hospital, where he was pronounced dead at 12:45 p.m. on Sept. 18, 1970." An autopsy found he died of asphyxia while intoxicated with barbiturates. One of those who attended his funeral was his friend, Miles Davis.

My feelings based on conversations I had with Jimi were that ultimately his death was caused by him being the "golden goose." His co-manager Michael Jeffery kept him out on the road and Jimi was exhausted and lost control of his life.

———

At Columbia Records, I enjoyed getting a regular paycheck and doing what I loved. Life was good. Now I could fix up my loft. I put up walls, a new oak floor, new kitchen and some built-ins. It was a lot of work, but worth it. Just as I started to kick back and relax, I got a call from John Sebastian, saying he needed a place to stay while doing some business in the city. The timing was perfect.

A little background. In addition to his music, John was now also known as the father of the 1960's tie-dye movement. The process of tie-dying clothing typically consists of folding, twisting, pleating or crumpling a piece of fabric and binding it with string or rubber bands. This is followed by application of one or more dyes.

John learned to tie-dye back at the Farm in Los Angeles from Ann Thomas (Tie-Dye Annie), who was a specialist in batik.

180

Sebastian shared this story in the interview for my book. "She encouraged me. She said your facility with your fingers makes you particularly good with this fold thing. I said 'Duh, I didn't know that I was good.' I went to the Farm in 1969 before Woodstock. I dyed all of those clothes. I started with just a white Levi suit. I started screwing around with the jacket. I went real slow and it just started to develop." John put the process on the map when he wore tie-dyed clothing at the Woodstock Festival that summer.

While I was away working on a project for Columbia, Sweet Apple, a San Francisco Sly Stone type Funk band, John began a tie-dying project in my loft. To put it mildly, he got a bit carried away. When I returned home, I found that every stitch of my clothing — including my underwear, socks and sheets — had been tie-dyed. Nothing was left untouched!

"Yeah, it happened at Harvey's," John recalled with a laugh. "I'd start a project...Maybe I'd have three colors. You realize you have red and blue and you could make a nice purple color. Now you have four colors. And maybe it gets to be a few more. By the end of all that, when you've tie-dyed your thing, there are cans of half-used-up dye.

"Maybe at Harvey's I was making something for somebody and there was all this left over dye. I've got his white underwear and white athletic socks and folded them up and dyed them as well. I was sort of sopping up the leftovers. Every now and then something really great would come out of the leftovers."

Meanwhile back at Columbia, as I mentioned earlier, the first artist I had signed was John Hall, a talented, multi-instrumental musician who did it all. On the West Coast, a potentially powerful group was gradually forming around Hall and I was producing an album with them. The group included Barry Tashian on guitar and vocals, Paul Harris on keyboards and Wells Kelley on drums.

As usual, band insanity took the spotlight away from the music. All went well until John Hall's wife, Johanna, overruled my choice of Barry Tashian as his second guitar and harmony singer. She felt it was her husband's album and it was therefore more important that John be the focus. Sadly, because of the dynamic with Johanna, the project went cold and didn't make it for Columbia. John would have his future success with his band, Orleans.

I produced some excellent R&B records at Columbia. One of the projects was a group called Sweet Apple, a five-piece funk band from San Francisco. They were a combination of Tower of Power and Sly & the Family Stone. While recording Sweet Apple at Wally Heider's San Francisco studio, the Jefferson Starship was also there working. During a break, I walked out of the studio and bumped into Paul Kantner, who grabbed my arm and pulled me into his *Blows Against the Empire* session. A wide range of musicians played on the album, which was a major hit and became a gold album. It's funny, I remember playing guitar, but I'm credited with playing bass. Who knows?

Meanwhile back in New York at Columbia, Songwriter/guitarist Dave Mason, bass player Carl Radle and drummer Jim Keltner were in town playing with Eric Clapton and Delaney and Bonnie. They came to visit me in the studio as I was working with R&B performer Bobby Lester and heard his tune "Freedom." They immediately offered to play on the track. Clive Davis loved the single "Sweet Gentle Nighttime" but it didn't take off and neither did Bobby.

All the releases had the OK from Clive at Columbia and we had a good rapport. I could have stayed at Columbia for years and had a good career as a staff producer. But I was getting frustrated. It was a combination of my usual wanderlust and not getting a hit from any of the funky records I was producing. My work was out of sync in color and sound with the company, and I had no real promotional backing. Single ads in *Billboard* magazine do not make a hit record.

It was quickly becoming apparent to me that I was more of a musician/writer/producer then one of the corporate guys. Many of the players I knew were moving to Woodstock and the artistic retreat was beginning to look interesting to me.

I sat down with Clive and told him how I was feeling. Clive told me he liked my work and if I had a project, the door was always open. I left on good terms. My days as a staff producer at Columbia were over. I walked out of Clive's office and headed down the hall to my office to collect my things. I stopped to tell Teo, Don DeVito and John Waxman, fellow Columbia producers and friends, that I was moving on. Then I left the building, grabbed a Sabrett hot dog from a cart on Sixth Avenue, took the F train downtown and turned that page of my life to my next chapter.

I had put a lot of energy into making my loft at 112 Greene Street a comfortable living space, but Woodstock was on my next page. Lots of the musicians and bands that I knew lived there behind the bushes. They included Bob Dylan, Paul Butterfield, members of The Band, John Sebastian, Dave Sanborn and many others. So I started staying with friends and spending time at the Bearsville recording studio, owned by Albert Grossman. At Bearsville, near Woodstock, I met Mike Lang, the co-creator of the Woodstock Music and Art Festival in 1969. Michael had just started a new label called Just Sunshine Records. We started hanging out and talking about possible ideas and projects.

Karen Dalton

One of the projects that Mike Lang talked about recording was the reclusive Karen Dalton. Karen had a serious drug problem and needed a patient but firm production technique. Mike knew of my experience with folk artists, including Dylan, Fred Neil and Richie Havens, among others. I had already met Karen through Fred Neil. Mike thought I would be the perfect producer for her. She was approached, the project came together, and we went into pre-production, with me starting to assemble the musicians and songs.

Karen was in love with the Paul Butterfield tune, "In My Own Dream," and wanted to go over to Paul's house and learn it from him. I spoke to Paul about us doing the tune and about Karen wanting to come over. He brought up Karen's drug and alcohol problems and offered to help. Ironically, we had a long conversation about musicians with drug problems, mainly Mike Bloomfield, because we both had worked with him and knew at that time he was slowly killing himself. The three of us got together at Paul's house and worked the tune out. This was the beginning of Karen's album, *In My Own Time*, now considered a cult classic.

Clean at the time and opposed to drug use as a bandleader, Paul couldn't understand how musicians could get themselves into that kind of problem. He had a home, wife and child in those days. He was the bandleader — the boss. He was responsible for the salaries of his band as well as the expenses. You pay the cost to be the boss and it gives you an alternative perspective. The band always gets paid first.

In later years, however, Paul Butterfield started drinking and doing heavy drugs himself, acting like the conniving "Back Door Man" in the tune by Willie Dixon. In the process, he lost his family, home and band. Albert Grossman, his manager at the time, had warned him about spending more money than he earned. Paul's story was that Albert was ripping him off. Albert was telling him the truth, but Paul couldn't hear him. It's a cliché, but this story has been repeated over and over. I have been there myself!

During the production of Karen's album, I was commuting back and forth between Woodstock and New York City. We recorded in studio A at Albert Grossman's Bearsville Studio, which had just been built with Mike Lang's Just Sunshine Records paying the bill. Karen's album, one of the first recorded there, took about six months to make, including a trip to San Francisco to add some horn parts.

In an interview for this book, Mike Lang recalled that the Karen Dalton recordings turned out to be an excellent album. "It got great critical acclaim and it has had a rebirth over the last few years. It wasn't easy to work with Karen's drug problem, but Harvey handled it well. That's Harvey's personality," Lang said. "He's very chilled out and easy to get along with. But he's bright and knows how to manipulate a situation. He did that with Karen."

For me, the key to working with Karen was to keep her confidence up and not let friends into the studio. I would give her as many options as possible without her having to choose one. We would always come to a conclusion together. I forced Karen to stretch out of her comfort zone so that she wouldn't fall into the predictable version of herself that her fans already knew. She knew I cared and gave me the performances I asked for. We selected the songs together and

185

discussed at great length her vocal approach with her having the final say. She left the choice of musicians up to me. We made great music together.

I have never received any producer royalties from Just Sunshine or Light in the Attic …… Just wondering.

The Fabulous Rhinestones

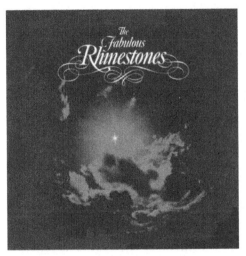

When I moved up to the Woodstock area, Greg Thomas, a San Francisco drummer, and I rented a converted barn off Highway 212 outside of Bearsville. We were only five minutes from the Bearsville recording complex.

I had been talking to Mike Lang about putting a band together. Greg suggested Kal David and Marty Grebb, who were friends of his from Los Angeles. We started talking to Kal about becoming part of the band.

About this time, the LA earthquake of February 1971 entered the equation. Because of the quake, Kal was ready to leave Los Angeles and so was Marty. The band was coming together. A friend from The Electric Flag days in San Francisco, Renol Andino, also joined us on percussion. Mike Lang was pleased with the line-up and offered to manage and sign the band to his label.

The Fabulous Rhinestones did three records for Lang's Just Sunshine label. The first album, *The Fabulous Rhinestones*, was recorded in the town of Oliverea at the Eagle Mountain House, which was an old inn we rented for the members of the band, their wives and girlfriends and the studio. It consisted of a trailer set between the house and 20 acres of woods. The engineer was Stan Goldstein, who worked for Lang at the Woodstock festival. We recorded the album during the winter, so there was lots of snow on the ground.

Since the control room was in the trailer next to the house, we'd do a few takes, then put our boots, winter coats and wool hats on and trudge through the snow to the trailer to listen.

One night, after finishing recording, we were sitting in front of the fireplace smoking joints at 2 a.m. with snow falling outside. We all decided that we needed good snow boots. So we made a band decision to drive six hours through a snowy blizzard to the 24-hour-a-day L.L. Bean store in Freeport, Maine. At 3:30 a.m., Stan, the only straight one in the group, drove us. We were toast by the time we got back, but we had boots!

I finally bought a house in Willow, about five miles north of Woodstock on Route 212. My next-door neighbor was Mark Harmon, who was one of the recording engineers at Bearsville. Next to him was Jim Rooney, who managed the studio. The house came with a horse stable on 10 acres, so I brought two horses to the new place and set up home. The outside stable became a popular spot at 5 a.m. in the morning, when my new neighbors would come by to help themselves to my horse manure at the side of the stable.

I added a mutt, named Trane, to my family of animals. Trane was a great dog but had an appetite for chickens. The Rooney's had a chicken coop that unbeknownst to me had become a favorite stop for Trane. One autumn afternoon around 4:30 p.m., I heard a yelping dog. I rushed outside to see what was going on and there was Trane running for his life with Rooney's wife, Sheila, hanging out of driver's side of her car swatting him with her broom. Trane survived that time. But, unfortunately, the dog's favorite pastime eventually caught up with him. Trane was eventually poisoned by one of the local farmers while raiding another chicken coop.

I converted my garage into a rehearsal studio, which at times was a local place to jam when my buddies dropped by. The usual cast included Paul Butterfield, John Sebastian, Jimi Hendrix, Rick Danko, Ian Hunter and Dave Sanborn.

One night, at about 4 a.m. in the dead of winter, I was sound asleep when there was pounding on the breezeway door. Rick Danko and Paul Butterfield, after consuming a load of vodka earlier at the Bear Café, came by to shoot bottles and write songs. We went out back with a .30-30 Winchester rifle and started shooting. It was hunting season, so hearing gunshots was not surprising to the local residents. But after a warning from the local police, we decided to go in the studio and play music.

That's when I found out the reason Danko and Butterfield were at my house at this ridiculous hour. They had both been caught cheating on their wives and were at the bar commiserating with each other. They had figured out that I had a place to play music and guns to shoot, so that was their next move in their drunken logic.

The next Rhinestones album, *Freewheelin'*, was produced by Bill Szymczyk at The Hit Factory in New York City. Bill was the producer of The Eagles, B.B. King, J. Geils, James Gang with Joe Walsh, and my bass instruction album, *How to Play the Electric Bass* for Elektra. We started recording in the early afternoon and by sunset we were ready to get some air and a bite to eat.

But first we all snorted a line of coke and then boisterously jumped into the elevator, literally bouncing off the walls. This caused the ancient Otis elevator to get stuck between floors. After pondering our situation, we began to yell for help. Then we heard a woman's voice from below telling us not to worry, help was on the way. The voice was Bonnie Raitt, who took out her guitar and serenaded us until help arrived.

Bonnie recalled that day in an interview for this book. "In the summer of 1974, I was recording my fourth album at the famous Hit Factory in Manhattan with R&B legend, Jerry Ragovoy, producing. One day I arrived at the studio, and as I walked in the door, I saw a half-dozen sets of legs, from the shins down. They were a few feet off the ground, where the elevator had apparently gotten stuck between floors.

"They started hollering for help as they heard me approach. I told them it was me and they said, 'Hey, Bonnie, it's the Fabulous Rhinestones. We've been stuck in here for hours...please go get some help!'

"Apparently the emergency call button didn't work. I don't remember how or who I got to help get them out, but I remember a lot of levity and joking around after — and surely relief. I'm sure it wasn't so funny when they were feeling trapped and uncertain when they'd get out.

"It's always been a great memory...especially as it had a happy ending. I don't know if I'd seen the band since we first met in Woodstock a couple of summers before while I was recording my second album at Bearsville Studios. Always loved the band and Marty Grebb went on to play with me for many years." As with many bands, the future of the Rhinestones was not bright. Greg Thomas got fired, Marty did not get along with Kal, and Kal did not get along with Marty. I had to choose between both of them and chose Kal. Marty and I continued our friendship until his recent passing.

The third album, *The Rhinestones,* was recorded at Bearsville Studios with new members. They included Eric Parker on drums, Bob Lienbach on keyboards and trombone and Arti Funaro on second guitar.

All three of these albums got rave reviews from critics and were played on progressive rock radio, though none sold in huge numbers. This was mainly because Just Sunshine Records didn't have the deep pockets to properly promote and distribute the releases and no hit single emerged. It was a vicious circle. You can't get one without the other.

The Fabulous Rhinestones

Just Sunshine Records Distributed by Famous Music Corporation · A Gulf+Western Company

Avoid Management/Deal Direct
One Gulf+Western Plaza
New York City 10023

We were a very tight band with a large cult following. We played on the same bill with The Allman Brothers, Stevie Wonder, The Doobie Brothers and Sly & the Family Stone. The group performed at a 1971 antiwar rally in New York City with John Lennon and Yoko Ono. But — like many, many bands — we were hampered by a lack of organization in business matters.

For example, to promote the first album, we performed in Los Angeles and got great radio play. Our recording of "What a

Wonderful Thing We Have" hit #78 on the **Billboard** charts, but our records weren't on the racks in the stores as the song was being promoted. When you get your shot and the people can't buy the music, everything falls apart. Paramount was the parent label and they did not give us the support we needed.

It was during the gig with the Rhinestones that I first met Steve Berkowitz, who was then a guitar player. He would later become a manager, producer and record company executive. Now he works on releasing the archives of Miles Davis, Bob Dylan, Leonard Cohen, Johnny Cash, Paul Simon and Robert Johnson.

"The Rhinestones were as great a band as any rock band who ever recorded," Berkowitz said in an interview for this book. "Those guys had an incredible band. Both on record and live, they were really fucking great! Kal David was a great guitar player, one of the greatest wah-wah pedal guys out there along with Hendrix. But he never quite got his due. And he was a great singer, too.

"I met Harvey when he was in the Rhinestones. It is not often that an artist of Harvey's vision and temperament comes along. A lot of people heard and saw that. Harvey wrapped it up. You can get lucky a couple of times, but after that there is something very real about it. And Harvey wrapped it up over and over and over. History shows us that."

Despite the praise and good words, the Rhinestones didn't make it. The group held together for two and half years. We played just about anywhere and everywhere we could get a gig — including colleges, clubs and bars.

When we started to feel like we had become Spinal Tap in the mid-seventies, we finally gave up. Kal went on to play with Etta James and Johnny Rivers. Marty Grebb played with Bonnie Raitt, Eric Clapton, Etta James and Leon Russell. Greg Thomas went on to play with George Clinton and Funkadelic, Taj Mahal, Loudon

Wainwright III and Roger McGuinn.

I stayed in Woodstock until 1976 doing session work.

The Joyous Lake

The Joyous Lake was a local music club in Woodstock created by Ron Marions and his flamboyant wife at the time, Velma. The club, located on Route 212 just as you entered downtown, featured wood, glass and a wide assortment of exotic plants.

It became the musical hub for Woodstock locals, which included Bob Dylan, Paul Butterfield, Levon Helm and John Sebastian. It was the place to check in when coming into town to record at Bearsville or a pit stop for musicians passing in the night. I remember many gigs that turned into jams that went on until the wee morning hours.

Marty Grebb and I were producing an album for singer/songwriter Kat McCord at Bearsville Studio. After the recording session was finished, we all drove down to the Joyous Lake to eat, drink and be merry. It was about 11:30 p.m. and we were primed for the evening jam, which included Howard Johnson, Dave Sanborn, Greg Thomas, Dennis Whitted, Kal David, Marty Grebb and myself. We were into it and when it came time for Howard Johnson's sax solo, he played a 45-minute piece examining every possible mode and relative mode of Herbie Hancock's "Cantaloupe Island." The audience went wild and kept buying the band drinks and we played till the sun came up. Then we, the denizens of the night, took to the road.

In 1973, in Woodstock on the corner of Route 212 and Wittenberg Road, in a small building across from Bearsville Records, a luthier opened up shop. His name was Steve Kalb (not related to Danny Kalb of The Blues Project). I met him while having dinner at the Bear Restaurant, which was part of Albert Grossman's music business complex. He had a couple of guitars he'd been working on

192

and invited me to check them out.

One was for Robbie Robertson, a member of The Band and then guitarist for Bob Dylan. Both guitars sounded great and I wanted one. We worked out the design specs for my guitar and Steve built it.

The instrument had an oval sound hole, shaped like Django Reinhardt's Selmer-Maccaferri guitar. It also had the pick guard and bridge with the same shaped cutaway as the guitar itself. The name-plate was in abalone on the 19th fret.

There is no truss rod running through the guitar, yet the neck has been true for over 41 years. I spent years looking for Steve Kalb and recently Chris Larson, a buddy in Tucson, creator of Girl Brand Guitars, told me that Kalb has become an entertainment attorney in Los Angeles.

Katz's Deli

Manny Katz opened a deli in downtown Woodstock (to my knowledge not related to the famous Katz's Deli in New York City). It was the daytime hot spot in town for all the countrified Jews and non-jews looking for a pastrami or corned beef sandwich.

Through the week, Katz's operated as a regular deli, but on Sundays a group of us "club members" would meet for brunch in the private dining space upstairs. Manny welcomed locals like Ron Marions, who owned the Joyous Lake, and Richie Fusco, who worked at Sunfrost, a local fruit stand, and musicians like myself. On occasion, Peter Max, the artist, would drop by. He had started to paint a mural on the upstairs ceiling from the top berth of the bunk bed. We called Peter the Michelangelo of Woodstock.

On these Sundays, Manny generously provided food and coffee which maintained us as we discussed personal matters, the state of the town, world politics, art, and of course music. For reasons unknown to me and the others, Manny had decided to close the deli. At our final Sunday brunch, Peter Max came in with a chain saw and cut out the ceiling area that he had been working on. He took it down the stairs through the deli to his van. I did not see him or the ceiling again until my wife Bonnie, who had worked on a project for Clairol cosmetics with him, reconnected us.

Peter Max and our friend Bob Ellis. Photo by Bonnie Brooks.

CHAPTER 18

Vignettes as a Bass Player

1970 — The Beatles Break-Up.

Making Bob Dylan's *New Morning*

One sunny afternoon in 1970, I was upstairs working on a painting — one that was inspired by some dying flies falling off the large picture window directly in front of me onto my already abstract canvas. The phone rang. It was Bob Dylan. He said he would stop by — if I was alone. I was.

We sat in my living room and started talking about what was going on in Woodstock. I made some coffee and as we talked, Dylan's eyes seemed to be capturing a picture of the room that stopped at the chessboard. I asked, "Do you play?" His answer came in his move to the table where my chessboard sat.

"I'll give you queen odds in the first game," I said. "If you win, we'll make it rook odds." We both laughed, lit up a joint and Bob made the first move across the board, with our back-and-forth repartee about our former manager, Albert Grossman.

Albert was an arrogant, sarcastic brilliant businessman with a nose for talent. He, as I wrote earlier in the book, managed Peter, Paul and Mary, Electric Flag, Janis Joplin, Richie Havens, Todd Rundgren, Bob Dylan and The Band. Most of his relationships ended bitterly.

After the game, I reminded Bob of the book he recommended to me as he was leaving a Greenwich Village bookstore and I was arriving titled, *The Death Ship*. He said, it's by B. Traven. It tells the story of an American sailor, stateless and penniless because he has lost his passport, who is harassed by police and hounded across Europe until he finds an "illegal" job shoveling coal in the hold of a steamer bound for destruction. B. Traven also wrote *Treasure of The Sierra Madre,* which John Huston made into a movie starring Humphrey Bogart.

A few weeks later, I got a call from Al Kooper booking me on a series of sessions for Bob's *New Morning* album, being recorded at Columbia Studio E. Prior to my being called for the session, Bob had gone through many players. They'd done a lot of recording in Nashville and New York, but still hadn't gotten the tunes the way Bob wanted them.

Al knew that we were all comfortable together and hoped that the sessions would go smoothly. There was a lot of burnt-out emotion in the studio when I got there, and I couldn't miss the frustration that Bob and Al were going through. The room was like sitting in a pressure cooker that was ready to blow! It took awhile for everyone to settle into a groove.

I played on "If Not for You," "Day of the Locusts," "One More Weekend," "Father of Night" and "The Man in Me." My performance is pretty much about the feel of the song. What I do is listen to a combination of the rhythm and chords and find a basic part that fits. Then I evolve the part as the song comes together. It's just moving and bridging sections so that the tunes become comfortable.

196

Jaco Pastorius

I got a call from my friend Jaco Pastorius, one of the greatest electric bass players. I first met Jaco one night after an Electric Flag in Greenwich Village at the Bitter End. He came backstage and told me I was his main inspiration when he was playing with Wayne Cochran and the C.C. Riders, a Florida R&B band. I would see Jaco around town or at gigs. Jaco heard that my father passed away and wanted to pay his respects. I told him that my Dad was buried in New Jersey, and that while I truly appreciated the gesture, the phone call was all that was needed.

Unfortunately, at this time in his life Jaco was suffering from drug and alcohol abuse and would not accept anything less than an actual visit to the cemetery. I gave him the address, and again repeated my appreciation of his friendship and that a trip there wasn't necessary, but he was determined. I thought it was very touching that Jaco wanted to pay his respects that way. Two or three days later I got a call from Joey Nardone, a mutual friend. He told me he had just bailed Jaco out of jail.

It seems that Jaco took a cab from Manhattan and after finally finding the cemetery, didn't have enough money to pay the cab driver. He got into an argument with the cabbie and was arrested. So Jaco never actually made it to my Dad's graveside but his respect will never be forgotten.

Jaco and I had strong mutual respect for each other. He had learned from my style and had evolved into the ultimate creative force on electric bass. So it was especially sad for me to witness the downfall of this amazing musician.

Butter's Last Tour

In 1985 Paul Butterfield was doing a tour cross-country and his manager Frank Yondalino called me up and asked if I wanted to put a band together for Butter's tour. I got Danny Dreher to play guitar and Crusher Green to play drums. It became obvious during rehearsals that Butter was strung out, but he seemed to have pulled himself together enough to leave town. Management scheduled a warm up gig at Tramps in Manhattan, a cozy jazz and blues bar with a small stage featuring an upright piano, which took up half the stage.

We sound checked in the afternoon and squeezed our drums and amps onto our half of the stage. At show time that evening, the bar was packed. Danny, Crusher and I walk onto the stage, start to tune up and get settled when we hear someone playing the piano. It was Jaco. He wanted to sing and play.

Before he could actually get into it Butter came running up and said to Jaco, "No one sings on my stage but me." He kicked Jaco off the stage. Jaco apologized and sat down against the back wall, maybe 15 feet from the stage. Butter kicks off the set and we burn. The crowd went wild and we did two encores.

Finally, everything quieted down and I sat with Jaco as he told me about his problems, which included paying alimony, two or three wives and lots of kids when he suddenly asked, "Can I try your bass?" I said sure. As he started to play, I turned on my cassette player, which was sitting on my bass amp. He played about twenty minutes of incredible jam. Our dinner of burgers arrived, and the moment ends.

Later that night I went over to the apartment Butter was then using. It was Butter and me talking about the gig and how good it sounded, but with some parts that had to be tightened up. There was a knock on the door and it was Jaco, bearing vodka, reefer and unbeknownst to me, some smack. So, after about an hour they were way further out than I ever wanted to be and I left. The band was leaving for the Midwest in the morning and was supposed to meet at Butter's apartment at 8 a.m. I got there in time to wait for the road manager to pour Jaco into a cab and throw Butter into the shower. We finally left at 4 p.m. as snow began to fall on the streets of New York City.

Levon Helm, John Belushi and the RCO All-Stars

It was New Years Eve, 1977, and my friend Levon Helm, drummer with The Band, was playing at the Palladium in Manhattan with his group, RCO All Stars. Though I had first met Levon when we played together at Forest Hills Stadium with Bob Dylan, we became close friends while living in Woodstock.

The All Stars had done two world tours and recorded a well received album. Steve Cropper and Donald "Duck" Dunn from Booker T. & the MG's, "Blue" Lou Marini, Tom "Bones" Malone (of Blood Sweat, & Tears, *Saturday Night Live* and David Letterman fame) and Juilliard-trained trumpeter, Alan Rubin, made one ass-kicking band.

The group was staying at the Gramercy Park Hotel on 21st Street and Lexington Avenue. Levon and Paul Butterfield exchanged road stories while getting in the mood for the evening's festivities. Levon seemed a little under the weather but was in the "show must go on" mode. I said my hellos and goodbyes and headed out to meet up downtown with Woodstock singer/songwriter Kat McCord. Then I picked up a bottle of Jose Cuervo and cabbed over to the Palladium to catch Levon's show.

When we arrived backstage, we bumped into *Saturday Night Live* comedian John Belushi, who had come in just before us. He spotted the bottle of tequila I was holding in a brown paper bag. "I'm introducing the band tonight and I could use some inspiration," John told us. We proceeded to drink Jose Cuervo until it was time for his introduction. He then staggered onto the stage and gave a glowing, if somewhat slurred, heartfelt intro.

The band kicked off the set and Belushi ran back over to us. "This band is fuckin' powerful," he said. For the next hour or so we watched and listened. Nothing was wasted. When Belushi and Dan Aykroyd formed the Blues Brothers, they recruited Booker T. & the MG's and the Saturday Night Horns at the Palladium.

At about 11:45 p.m., the show was over. The audience seemed a little disorientated having anticipated New Years Eve with Levon and the RCO All-Stars. Instead they were ushered out onto the cold and windy Manhattan streets to celebrate on their own. We joined the audience exiting to the street and shared their bewilderment for a couple of minutes. Then we grabbed a cab and went over to the Gramercy Park Hotel in time to celebrate New Years Eve.

Seals and Crofts – *Summer Breeze*

In 1970, I first recorded with Seals and Crofts in San Francisco on their album, *Down Home*. Producer John Simon and I had recorded together on many projects and he thought I would be the right bass player for Dash and Jimmy on some of the tunes. The tunes I played on were "Purple Hand," "Hollow Reed," "Gabriel Go on Home" and "Cotton Mouth."

Though the album was not a major hit, playing with Seals and Crofts was, for me. I don't think they ever wrote a bad song. Every song has a meaningful lyric, is fun to play as a musician and is ear candy to the listener. Their music is so melodic that my bassline played itself. As you can tell, I'm a big fan.

By the time the sessions were over, Jimmy Seals, Dash Crofts and I were musically locked. To this day Dash and I still keep in touch. In 1972, I received a call from producer Louie Shelton asking me to fly out to Los Angeles to record on Seals and Crofts' next album, *Summer Breeze.*

Jimmy and Dash picked me up at the airport at around 6 p.m. Over dinner, we talked about the spiritual aspect of the music as well as the lyrics. We also discussed the essence of their Bahia faith and the role it played in the creation of the music we were about to record.

After eating, we got down to the music. Sitting there and listening to their harmonies bare bones, with no studio effects, really helped me find the pathway through their music. I wrote out a chord chart for myself for "Summer Breeze" and defined the structure of the song. It started with a thematic lick/verse/chorus/2x. The second time the lick is a vocal lick/bridge/VV/CC/ lick out. Jimmy and Dash made the music seem so easy and natural. Everything fit right into place. The song was ready for the studio. The other musicians were all top LA session players and I was the only east coast representative. Two of the tunes I played on became hit singles, "Summer Breeze" and "Hummingbird."

I had first heard drummer Jim Keltner playing with Hungarian American guitarist Gabor Szabo and then with Delaney and Bonnie, but the "Summer Breeze" session was the first time we played together. We had an hour lunch break coming up. I was ready to go out and find a sandwich or something when Keltner came up to me and grabbed my arm saying you got to meet Buckwheat. We walked a couple of blocks up Cohuenga Boulevard and stopped at this small but jam-packed Drum Shop. We walked in, walked through to the back of the shop and up some stairs through an open door into Buckwheat's studio. Buckwheat was David Wheat and it was his studio and Drum Shop. An amazing feature of this studio was that the whole drum set except for the bass drum were suspended from the ceiling making it a challenge just to play. Jim somehow made those drums work but I on the other hand couldn't get Wolfgang Melz, who was jamming on the bass, to give it up and let me play.

Gospel Music with Fontella Bass, 1995

I got a call from Stew Cutler, a friend and guitarist, who wanted me to play on a gospel record that Fontella Bass was making. Her R&B hit, "Rescue Me," had charted in the Top 10 in 1965. Now Fontella was getting ready to record her new gospel album called *No Ways Tired* for Nonesuch Records. This was my first gospel session. Fontella was a great lady and amazing to work with. Every song had its twist and her feel was the key ingredient.

In gospel music, the keyboard, usually the piano or the Hammond B3 organ, sets the feel or mood of the song. The left hand of the player plays a bassline that directs the rhythm and the harmony. What I played had to incorporate the keyboard part into my bassline so that our lines would not conflict. Since both of our parts were in the same range, I either duplicated the keyboard part or abbreviated his line with my own rhythmic phrasing mostly dominated by the root and fifth of each chord.

So much of the R&B I had learned growing up came from gospel music. Experiencing the roots of the music and the people who created it has greatly added to my palette of musical colors. Some gospel artists I recommend listening to include the Staple Singers, The Dixie Hummingbirds, the Mighty Clouds of Joy and BB and CC Wynans.

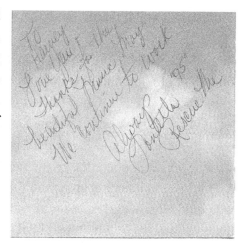

Lessons with Dave Holland

When I played with Miles Davis on his *Bitches Brew* album, I shared the bass chair with Dave Holland and on one session Ron Carter. After the sessions, I started taking lessons with Dave to get some of his thinking into my head. He taught me about the Gamala Taki system for understanding and creating complicated rhythms.

This technique had me breaking all the rhythmic phrases into threes and twos using the words. GaMaLa, threes and TaKi, twos. For example, 4/4 would be:

```
4/4 (8/8) Ga Ma La Ta Ki Ga Ma La -
5/4       Ga Ma La Ta Ki Ga Ma La Ta Ki Ta Ki
           1      2     3      4     5
```

Using these sounds unlocked my western music paralysis. This knowledge really applies to Indian and Middle Eastern music, which I am now surrounded by living here in Jerusalem.

Jamming with Jack DeJohnette

One of my favorite drummers is Jack DeJohnette. I played with him on *Bitches Brew* and shortly after he moved to Woodstock, New York in about 1975. Once settled into his new home, he called and wanted me to give him the lowdown on Woodstock. I invited him over to see my studio and gave him the basic information of who, what, when and where the music happened in the town.

While reminiscing about the *Bitches Brew* sessions, I asked him if I could take some lessons with him. He invited me to come over to his house and play. I had imagined he would show me some stuff.

When I got to his home, he took me down to his basement studio where we just began to play. He did not speak one word about music. Jack switched from drums to piano and back again while I played my Fender Bass. The lesson, in retrospect, was about both mental and physical endurance.

As I wrote earlier, one of the major music clubs in the Woodstock area was The Joyous Lake. We all used to get together to jam there regularly. Through the owner, Ron Marions, I had set up a jam with DeJohnette and myself with Kal David on guitar, Dave Sanborn on alto sax and Marty Grebb on keyboard.

In my opinion, Jack is one of the music world's greatest drummers, bassists and piano players. On that night, he set the bar high and we all had to push ourselves to meet his lofty standard. His performance perfectly fit #10 of my commandments — play with musicians that challenge you.

CHAPTER 19

The Meltdown

1977: President Carter pardons draft evaders in the Vietnam War.

By the mid 1970s, The Fabulous Rhinestones had come to an end. I began a phase of my life that would end up a few years later in a personal meltdown. It wasn't for a lack of work — it was far too much work with endless projects, some good some bad.

In Woodstock, I worked on an album with the songwriter Robert Lee, that began at the Bearsville Studio in Woodstock and finished at Axis Sound Studio in Atlanta, Georgia. While recording in Atlanta, one of the owners of Axis, Mike Hendry, was impressed with my credits and my work and offered me the position of studio manager. The job came with a decent paycheck which came in handy during the disco era that put a lot of bass players out of business. Increasingly, synthesized bass parts were used to create robotic dance grooves.

At the time, I saw the position as an opportunity to record my own music and to learn how to run a recording studio while I waited out the demise of disco. In hindsight, my move to Atlanta may have been a mistake since it took me out of the first call list of top session players in New York and Los Angeles. I worked at Axis Studio for two years, booking pop groups such as Kansas and talented musicians, like Duck Dunn, who was the bassist for Booker T. & the

MG's. Though I was playing locally, my wanderlust had set back in.

Singer/guitarist Lonnie Mack who had a big hit with an instrumental version of the Chuck Berry hit "Memphis" in 1964, was in Atlanta doing some work. He heard I was at the studio and came over to meet me. When he arrived, we walked into the studio and sat around the grand piano, which was in the center of the room under a spotlight. It was kind of spiritual. Lonnie and I sat by that piano and began talking. He told me what he was doing and asked what it was like in Atlanta. I told him the truth — I was busy with work, but I was starting to miss the excitement of an ass-kicking band.

He began telling me about a project he was working on with Ed Labunski, the award-winning New York City jingle writer whose claim to fame was the commercial, "This Bud's for You." Labunski, Mack said, was tired of doing commercials and wanted to write and play music. He was going to build a studio in rural Pennsylvania near Milford on the upper Delaware River. They were looking for a bass player. Mack invited me to join the group.

I gave my notice, packed up my van and took up off for Milford, Pennsylvania. When the construction of the studio began in 1980, I recruited my brother Gary, who is also a musician, to assist in building the studio and to become the studio engineer.

The first album out of the stable was going to be a new country-western swing band, called South. Ed and Lonnie hired a female vocalist named Trudy, who lived in Texas. She was moving to Milford with her belongings and needed help driving cross country. Neither Ed nor Lonnie wanted to make the drive, so I was recruited.

I flew to Texas and rented a truck with a tow rig that would pull her 1957 Oldsmobile with her belongings to Milford. Trudy was a Texas cowgirl from Walnut Springs Texas, a town with a population of about 850 people. It was out there in the middle of gigantic Texas. She was my first cowgirl country singer and I was her first New York

Jew. Blonde hair and freckles as I remember. She was friendly and funny.

As we progressed on the long road trip, Trudy and I became romantically involved. By the time we reached Milford, we were an item. This didn't sit well with Ed Labunski. After a month, he fired both of us.

Trudy came with me back to Atlanta, where we proceeded to put a new band together. From Atlanta, we sent demo tapes to Labunski and he offered to sign us to his label. The group included Bobby Faris on guitar and Joey Dukes on drums. So we went back to Milford. On our second day back, while setting up at the studio, we received the news that Ed Labunski had been killed after smashing his car head-on into a tree while driving from New York City to Milford. It was rumored that while focusing on snorting some cocaine, he skidded on an ice patch and lost control of the car.

After Labunski's death, everything went up in smoke, including my relationship with Trudy. My brother, Gary, and his wife, Jodi, were living in a house near the studio with Harmony, my niece, who was just a toddler at the time. They invited me to move in while I figured out what my next move would be.

My sister-in-law, Jodi, was ahead of her time. She was into natural gardening and raising chickens for eggs and meat. I became part of their everyday family farming life with my brother. Gary learned how to slaughter chickens. I can tell you first-hand that when you cut off the head of a chicken, they actually do run around for awhile.

My leaving New York City and moving to Atlanta blew the momentum I had built as a studio bass player over the years. I was back to bouncing from band to band. I played about a year with Clarence Clemons and the Red Bank Rockers. The gig was well paid and going great, until a new producer took over and fired the entire rhythm section — bringing in his own players. This is not a unique story in the music business. As a producer, I have done the same thing myself. However, being on the receiving end is not sweet.

In 1985, I went on the road with Paul Butterfield. It would be his last tour. Paul was not in good health at the time. Beginning in 1980, he underwent several surgical procedures to relieve his peritonitis, a serious and painful inflammation of the intestines.

Frank Yondalino, Butterfield's manager at that time, asked me to put together a band to play around Paul. I hired guitarist Danny Dreher and drummer Crusher Green. The tour was tough — in fact, brutal. We were in the middle of a bitter, cold winter in Colorado and traveled in a freezing, uncomfortable van working our way slowly to Spokane, Washington and then back again. Although Butterfield had been opposed to hard drugs as a bandleader (and talked of it often), he was now addicted to drugs and alcohol and had been for quite some time.

On the tour, he was using painkillers and heroin, topped off with alcohol. This would eventually take his life. Though we got some good reviews along the way, the tour was a grueling challenge for me. I knew deep in my soul that my time on road trips like this was coming to an end.

CHAPTER 20

After the Crash

1988: Compact Discs outsell vinyl records for the first time.

After a six-month stint with the Butterfield Blues Band in the dead of winter, I crashed and hit bottom. I was 45 years old, toasted and burnt to a crisp living with my mother in Queens. My body was physically and mentally exhausted.

My whole life had been consumed by music. Music had been the motivation behind all I did as a young man. Being single without attachments, I could move around and live anywhere very easily. Everything I needed was in my car. But the world was changing and it was becoming harder to survive economically.

Now, I was lonely. I spent a lot of time in bookstores by myself and at night playing gigs in bars. Many people around me had heavy drug and alcohol problems. They were now having heart attacks and other serious health issues. I knew instinctively that I was headed in that direction as well.

In 1986 there was an unsuccessful attempt to resurrect The Electric Flag in Los Angeles by manager/promoter Ray Paret. The new version of the group, featuring Mike Finnegan, Kal David, Louie Biancello, David (Lefty) Foster and the Phenix Horns with Buddy Miles and myself, sounded great but the reunion failed after drummer/vocalist Buddy Miles, who had just gotten out of jail, made a speech at a rehearsal telling the band how much he loved everyone and how we would be the greatest band. I knew Buddy well and understood his jive when I heard it. I was waiting for the other shoe to drop. It did. The next day, Buddy abruptly left to join Santana. Without Buddy, there was no Electric Flag.

At my mother's apartment, I sacked out in bed and slept, slept and slept some more. With no new work on the horizon, I went back to playing club gigs, where I had begun. One was Crazy Horse in New Rochelle, which opened in 1980 and was run by Vinnie Pastore, who would later become "Big Pussy" on the HBO television series, *The Sopranos*. Vinnie has always been a big music fan and had followed my career going back to *Super Session*. The Crazy Horse became a steady gig for me.

Vinnie recalled how it came about in an interview for this book. "We had a lot of live music at the Crazy Horse," he said. "One night, Lester Chambers (of the Chambers Brothers fame) was in the club. He sat in with Harvey and they formed the Lester Chambers-Harvey Brooks band right there on my stage. It was a night I will never forget.

"We became friends and would talk endlessly about movies, music and life in general. Harvey would play 'Harvey's Tune' for me during his gigs. Harvey could play with anybody. He is up there with Jaco (Pastorius) and all the great bass players. He's Harvey Brooks! When I talk with people about bass players, they say 'Harvey Brooks! He's a legend.'"

Vinnie and me were down in the basement of the Crazy Horse after I had just gotten back from a gig in the Virgin Islands and had put this band together with my brother Gary on sax, Stew Cutler on guitar, Danny Louis on keys and trumpet and Gary Gold on drums. It was great playing with my brother Gary. He was playing keyboards and sax and burned.

We were talking about our futures as we saw it. Vinnie loved the club, but he wanted to get into acting and either his brother or cousin was connected in the business. I wanted to get a kick-ass band together. We smoked a couple of joints as we were talking and then I went upstairs to play my set.

We started playing "Mustang Sally" and about three minutes into it I see out of the corner of my eye that Vinnie's pushing this tall guy up on stage. And then Vinnie grabs the mic and says, "Harvey, meet Lester Chambers from the Chambers Brothers." And then Lester grabbed the mic, started singing and as Vinnie said, that was the beginning of the Chambers-Brooks Band.

At the end of the set Lester got a cowbell and started his signature tune, "Time Has Come Today" which was a huge hit, and the audience went nuts. After the show Vinnie, Lester and I sat at the bar as Vinnie poured rounds of tequila and we saluted the new band.

Between the band with Lester Chambers and occasional gigs with the "Shaboo All Stars" with front man David "Lefty" Foster, I made enough to pay my bills. I was getting by — just barely.

One day my phone rang. A bright and cheery voice asked, "Are you the same Harvey that went to Van Buren High School with my brothers, Lloyd and Morey Ruza?" I answered yes.

"My name is Bonnie Behar, but you would probably remember me as Bonnie Ruza." Remember! I had a serious crush on her in junior high school and at Martin Van Buren High School, when she signed her picture in my yearbook, "Love, Bonnie."

At Van Buren High, Bonnie only dated college guys and was way out of my league. Now, she told me, she was the marketing/media/director for the Museum of Arts and Sciences & Industry in Bridgeport, Connecticut (now The Discovery Museum) and was putting together an exhibit called "Rock 'n' Roll Art & Artifact" with co-curator, Bob Ellis.

She had gotten my name and phone number from Frank Sanzo,

the owner of "The Rocking Chair", a bar I played at who had responded to an ad that she had put into the Connecticut newspapers to acquire music memorabilia from the 1960s. We chatted for a while about my life, her divorce and her three daughters. She told me that her favorite tune was Seals and Croft's "Summer Breeze," on which I had played bass. We set up a time to meet in Manhattan. I had a recording session at Sony and was carrying my electric bass when we met in the lobby. Bonnie thought all bass players played upright instruments and did not recognize me holding what she thought was a guitar.

Right off the bat, we had different frames of reference. Bonnie suggested that we talk over lunch and I suggested Wolf's Deli, a favorite of mine.

For me, it was love at first sight — 25 years after high school. Bonnie didn't know about my school crush and I didn't mention it. She told me about the exhibition that she was putting together. It was weak on historical items from the 60s and she hoped that I would be willing to share my collection of memorabilia with the museum for several months. I was playing in Connecticut on Saturday night and said I would stop by on my way home from the gig on Sunday to share what I had in my archives.

My stash included gold records, posters and photos. The original plan was for me to stop by her house in Westport the morning after a gig. I called her Sunday morning to say that the morning would not work since I had gone back to Queens on Saturday night. I wanted to know if it would be okay to come by on Sunday evening instead. Our story together starts here.

It was a cold rainy day the last weekend of October as I drove up the Merritt Parkway to Westport. The leaves were crisp and colorful with a bit of a bite in the air. Her home was warm and her daughters, Celia and Julie, added their own flavor to the dinner she had prepared. Her oldest, Lori, was already studying at Georgetown University in Washington, D.C.

I remember at the time saying to Bonnie, who was looking right at me, that I didn't do well with a lot of hugging or commitment. I was trying to protect myself emotionally. She rolled her sultry green eyes, affirming that she thought I was nuts!

But that rainy afternoon, I met my soul mate — the person I would marry. Amazingly enough, she felt the same way about me. We started to date and it was serious for both of us. However, the process wasn't instant or smooth. Bonnie was concerned about her girls. They were used to living alone with their mom in a girl's dormitory. How would they feel about me — a bearded, long-haired musician, spending time with their mom in Westport?

I had a winter gig set up in St. Croix. I was supposed to come by to say goodbye before I left but didn't. Needless to say, she was pissed and wished me a not-so-fond farewell. I called and coerced her to fly down St. Croix, which she did. When she was there, I was a pot smoking, liquor drinking, cocaine sniffing, selfish human being.

Bonnie got a good wide shot of my life on this trip and told me she would have to leave. She said I was a nice guy, but the kind of life I was living would not fit into her family or the home that she had spent years putting together. As she was walking out the door, I said I would give it all up. And I did! I quit cold turkey. I did not want to lose this amazing woman and swore I would change.

———

When I met Bonnie, she was a divorced mom simultaneously wearing many hats. Not only was she the Marketing/Media Director for the Discovery Museum in Bridgeport Connecticut, she was also the

Cablevision Access Coordinator for Westport covering arts and politics in the Fairfield County area. In addition to that, she freelanced as a producer and production manager for several film and video companies in New York City and Connecticut. But she was a mom first and loved it!

Harvey and Bonnie Brooks at the Rock & Roll: Art & Artifacts show, 1989

The Discovery Museum is the largest interactive arts and science museum between New York and Boston. The rock exhibit covered the relationship between art, science and industry in rock 'n' roll, covering the growth of the music from the 1950s thru the 1980s. The exhibit included Linda McCartney's photos, Andy Warhol's paintings and poster art, photos by Annie Leibovitz, works by Robert Mapplethorpe, Keith Haring and paintings by Ron Wood. Also on exhibit was Jimi Hendrix's guitar and clothing.

Richie Havens was the highlight performer of the opening event. I put some musicians together to provide additional background music. Guests at the event also included Meatloaf and The Average White Band, as well as Keith Haring. The show was a major success.

———

I was now living with Bonnie in Westport, putting down my Connecticut roots and continuing to do local gigs. While on a bathroom break at a gig with David Foster's Shaboo All Stars, I noticed blood in my urine. I told Bonnie about it and she brought me to my doctor who treated the bleeding as a urinary tract infection. He mentioned that men do not usually get urinary tract infections, so he referred me to a urologist named Dr. Eugene Birns. He scheduled me for surgery after a cystoscopy found a tumor on my bladder which was diagnosed as bladder cancer. The tumor was removed with clean margins, so I did not have to do any treatment.

My surgery was done at Mt. Sinai Hospital in New York City. I was lying in bed with a catheter and a drip on a tripod with Bonnie watching over me. My hospital roommate, an elderly man with Alzheimers, shared his magic tricks at my bedside while in his hospital gown. This bizarre scene was straight out of a Woody Allen or Mel Brooks comedy!

Bonnie had been with me all day. As it was getting dark outside, she opted to go back to Westport to be with her girls, who were being watched by a friend. On leaving, Bonnie reminded me to question the nurses to be sure that I was getting the correct care. I could tell she was concerned as she left the hospital. Bonnie had witnessed problems when she worked years ago in Santa Barbara as a lab technician at Sansum Medical Clinic. She knew firsthand what can happen in hospitals, and unknowing to me, had been acting as my patient advocate.

Her warning was accurate. As I was falling asleep, a nurse

entered the room to change my drip. I woke up in the morning and my left hand was as big as a baseball catcher's mitt. The nurse had not inserted the needle into a vein, but directly into my arm. Freaked out, I called Bonnie, who got into her car and drove to Manhattan and had me discharged immediately.

Bonnie's home with her girls was not only a dormitory but housed a menagerie of pets which included, cats, dogs, vermin and a bird. These ladies had their routines set in a non-male environment. Bonnie had previously kept her social life out of the house and suddenly I appeared. She had been alone for over 10 years and I was a musician who had been on the road his entire life. I was forty-six years old. Bonnie's oldest daughter Lori was enrolled at Georgetown University and my presence was like an alien invasion to her daughters Celia, fourteen and Julie, eleven years old.

Celia, who has a masters in guidance counseling, is now in her mid 40s, a life coach and author of a website for moms. She laughingly recalled those days when she and her sister, Julie, resisted their mom's new boyfriend when he came into their home. "When Harvey arrived, there was an immediate resistance. I remember a time when my sister and I were doing the laundry. We freaked out when we saw Harvey's underwear in there. We had a moment of pure terror. We were screaming and throwing his underwear back and forth at each other."

I tried to win the girls over with my rock history, only to be told by Julie, "Oooh, you play old people's music." And when I told Celia I had played with Miles Davis, she told me she didn't know who he was. "He started rattling off the names of people trying to impress me and I didn't know who any of them were," she said. But the one she did know was Bob Dylan. She was a big fan who had attended several of Bob's concerts with her friends.

My car at the time was a 20-year-old wood-paneled green four-on-the-floor Dodge station wagon. It was an extreme embarrassment for the girls. Bonnie worked during the day and I gigged at night. During the day, I would drive Julie and her friend, Lee, to middle school. They thought of me as the John Candy character, Uncle Buck.

They would duck down in the back of the car until I pulled up at the school, and then they jumped out, running up the stairs as I drove away.

"I'm sure Harvey left this out," recalled Celia, looking back. "That old station wagon was filled with junk in the back. We were already not wealthy and lived in Westport, which is such an affluent place. We were the kids who had no money. Having your stepdad drop you off in a beater wood-paneled green station wagon that was filled with garbage in the back was awful.

"Harvey hoarded stuff in that car. Like record albums, clothing, candy bars and food wrappers. Sometimes there were ants. He went to gigs in it. It was before my mom made him stop eating crap. My mom eventually shaped him up."

Celia said it took her about six months to bond with Harvey, while Julie took over two years. "In our family, Harvey became sort of the drug and alcohol police. My mom never drank or did any drugs at all. So, whenever she suspected that my sister and I were drinking or smoking pot, she would send Harvey in to assess the situation.

"We became really good at hiding what we were drinking. Our house butted up against really dense woods, and we'd throw the empties out the back window. When my parents sold the house, they were cleaning up outside and found the empties graveyard. It was only then, that they realized what we'd done."

One incident Celia clearly remembered helped define her relationship with Harvey. "I was in college and came home one night from visiting a girlfriend on a break and definitely had been smoking pot. I reeked of cigarettes and pot, which my mom knew and hated. When I came in, my eyes were bloodshot and my mom took one look at me and said my eyes would not look that way if I hadn't been smoking pot with my girlfriend. She was furious.

"I said I don't know what you are talking about. I'm not high, I wasn't smoking pot. It's just my allergies. She called Harvey and asked him to check me out. He got right in my face and made me blow on him. I was reeking of pot and I know he knew that.

"Harvey sort of looked at me and then at my mom and said 'No, she didn't smoke pot. She's not high.' My mom immediately said she was sorry for accusing me. Harvey said he thought she was smelling incense. My mom then left the room.

"When she left, Harvey looked at me and said: 'Tomorrow night, I want Burger King. I want a Double Whopper with cheese and everything on it. I want French fries and a chocolate shake. You can leave it at the top of the stairs in the basement.' My mom wouldn't let him eat that stuff anymore, so I had to sneak it into him."

Shortly after my surgery, Bonnie and I decided to get married. Celia was OK with it, but Julie wasn't. Julie wanted to know why Bonnie couldn't just live with me. Both girls said they did not want to become the "Brady Bunch!" We forged ahead anyway and planned our backyard garden wedding for June 11, 1989.

In a conversation about who we would invite to the wedding Bonnie told me about an artist friend who lived down the road and was an interesting character. He was an incredible artist/painter who could always be found with a cup of coffee in his hand. She told me his name was Eric Von Schmidt. It turned out that I knew Eric from my folk days and I said, that wasn't coffee in his cup. Bonnie had no idea Eric was a musician.

Von Schmidt's father, Harold von Schmidt, was a famous Western illustrator who did illustrations for the Saturday Evening Post. Eric began selling his own artwork while he was still a teenager. Following a stint in the army, he won a Fulbright scholarship to study art in Florence. He moved to Cambridge, Massachusetts, in 1957, where he painted and became part of the coffeehouse scene.

With Eric Von Schmidt, Bonnie and Bob Ellis at the wedding

I had first met Eric in 1964 while I was playing bass with Folk Singer Tom Rush at the Club 47 in Cambridge. Tom introduced me to Eric with whom he revived and arranged the traditional song "Wasn't That a Mighty Storm?" about the 1900 hurricane that destroyed Galveston, Texas. Among his best known and performed original compositions is the song "Joshua Gone Barbados" which depicts Ebenezer Joshua, the head of a labor union and head of the government of Saint Vincent (island), vacationing during a time of labor strife leading indirectly to the deaths of three men.

Eric created album covers for Joan Baez, Cisco Houston, John Renbourn, Reverend Gary Davis, Geoff and Maria Muldaur, James Baldwin's readings as well as the 1965 Bob Dylan Joan Baez concert tour poster. Four years before his death, von Schmidt painted his last epic of American history. The canvas' subject was of Lewis and Clark's Corps of Discovery honoring its bicentennial.

In later years my amazing wife Bonnie put a surprise birthday party together for me. Because people couldn't park on Compo road where our house was, Eric offered up his house and Bocce Court which was right behind ours. Keith Richards, Danny Kortchmer, Charlie Karp, Jim Rooney, family and friends gathered on Eric's Bocce court to throw the balls. While jamming at the party, Eric and I came up with an idea that grew into a song called "China." We recorded it in our basement studio and has never been released. I believe this song we wrote may have been the last song he wrote before going back to painting full time.

About a month after my surgery, Bonnie had discovered a lump on her breast that was diagnosed as Stage 2 breast cancer. She had her first surgery right before the wedding, understanding that she would also require treatment with chemo and radiation. All the excitement of the wedding planning was shadowed by the reality of yet another surgery that would have to be dealt with after the wedding.

Bonnie had suggested that I jump ship, since her survival was questionable and the situation with the girls would not be easy. Bonnie also thought a wedding under her circumstances would be a waste of money. It was a bit of a battle. But we went forward with our plans. Our wedding was on a beautiful sunny Sunday morning.

My mother was thankful that finally, at 46 years old, I was getting married. To my mom, it meant I would have some stability.

Bonnie and I shared our commitment with a very large community of friends and family. I broke the glass and kissed my new bride under the Chuppah. My musician friends, including my brother, Gary, Baron Raymonde, Danny Louis, Stew and Mary Jean Cutler, David "Lefty" Foster, Angel Rissoff, Billy Reed, Bob Lienbach and John Simon, would make up the wedding band.

While in treatment, Bonnie continued to work for the museum, Cablevision, and as a freelance producer. She never took time off. Fridays were chemo days, knowing that most of the unpleasant side effects would be over by Monday.

Bonnie knew that my night vision was not very good, so she would drive me to my evening gigs, which started about 10 p.m. in New York City. We would get home at 3 or 4 a.m. and Bonnie was up to get the girls to school and herself to work. Her inner strength during those difficult days was unbelievable.

My stepdaughter Julie who was 11 when I moved in with Bonnie, passed away on April 10, 2018 from Stage 4 colon cancer. She was 42 and left behind four children. It was a heart-rending situation for all of us.

Julie was the youngest of Bonnie's three daughters. Of the three girls, Lori, Celia and Julie, Julie and I had spent the most time together in Westport and Tucson. I loved her as if she was my own birth child. I can't begin to fathom Bonnie's pain at the loss of her youngest child.

During those early years, when Bonnie was either producing or editing during the day, I was responsible for Julie after school. Julie's biological father, who lived 10 minutes from us, never spent any real time with her. His idea of an outing was to take her to the dentist!

It took me awhile to connect with Julie. She resented me taking over her spot in her mother's bed. She looked at me like I was the Creature from the Black Lagoon. What brought us together was a job that took Bonnie to England. While she was gone, Julie and I would go out to eat a lot and she felt she had me wrapped around her little finger, which she did.

Julie was totally unimpressed by my rock 'n' roll pedigree until some of her friends became Jim Morrison and The Doors fans. My cassettes, that I couldn't impress her with before, started to vanish. All of a sudden I was cool!

Julie grew up, got married and mothered three wonderful children with her first husband, Arin, in Tucson. Her Daniel, the love of her life and the father of two-year-old Adam, never let her down. Julie was a uniquely funny compassionate person who as a social worker rescued abused children from dysfunctional homes.

CHAPTER 21

Marriage and Music

1996: About 45 million people use the Internet, with roughly 30 million of them in North America.

Westport, Connecticut — about an hour's drive from New York City — is considered the Hollywood of the East. The town is a beach community filled with a wide spectrum of upper crust talent that includes artists, writers, filmmakers and the heads of major corporations.

Several months into my life in Connecticut, I got a call from Gary Gold, a drummer I had mentored out of heroin addiction years before. He was putting a band together with Jimmy Vivino and wanted to know if I would like to play bass? I said yes.

We started out as a trio playing small New York City clubs. As our following began to grow, we added more musicians including Kevin Bents on keyboard and Jerry Vivino, Jimmy's brother, on sax. We took the name The Little Big Band. Eventually, our home base became Hades, an uptown club on 96th Street and Second Avenue. We played there every Tuesday night and steadily grew in size, adding three additional horn players.

We became a scene, with notable players beginning to drop in to jam. The audience included record producers and celebrities like Bill Murray and his brother Sean. Steady participants included Phoebe Snow, Donald Fagen, Jeff Young, Catherine Russell and on occasion, Michael McDonald, Boz Scaggs and Cindy Lauper. Phoebe Snow would get up on stage and blow the audience away with "Midnight Hour" and "634-5789." One winter night, Sally Grossman, Albert's wife, brought down a bus load of friends and musicians from Woodstock, which included Rick Danko, Levon Helm, Garth Hudson and Jimmy Wieder.

At Hades, I met Pete Fogel the publisher of "Metal Leg/the Steely Dan Magazine" who asked if he might interview me for his magazine. That was the beginning of a long ongoing friendship.

We accumulated a large following that now overflowed the small club. When the city closed down Hades, we became a band on wheels playing at several notable clubs, including the Lonestar Cafe, the China Club and Le Bar Bat. Bonnie and I would get to whatever club it was early enough for me to set up, grab a table and order some dinner, which was part of my paycheck. On one of those evenings at Hades, when I took to the stage, I watched Bonnie invite a guy who had no place to sit over to our table. After we wrapped, I walked over to find Bonnie sitting with Donald Fagen, one of the founders of Steely Dan.

Not being from the world of rock, I knew immediately she had no idea who Fagen was. She was just sitting there chatting with a stranger. Fagen had dropped by to check out the band. Bonnie and Fagen were, believe it or not, in a discussion about medicated Band-Aids and a new type of razor blades with soap that he had discovered. I shook my head in amazement, acknowledged Fagen and started packing up my bass and amp to leave.

After the Hades gigs, Bonnie and I had a 3 a.m. ritual of getting some Fig Newtons, black licorice and coffee from the next door 24-hour Pakistani market for our ride back to Connecticut. We went next door to the bodega, where we saw Fagen again, this time standing on line. He immediately pointed out the razors, which had some kind of slime that acts as a lubricant. Cool, I thought, promptly buying the Fig Newtons and coffee and leaving for home. Once in the car, I asked Bonnie if she knew who that guy was that she had been talking to. "I thought he looked like an accountant or a Wall Street guy," she said, totally clueless.

The following Tuesday, Donald returned, this time to sit-in with the band. He started to show up every Tuesday. We in The Little Big Band were pleased to see that he was comfortable playing with us. The first Steely Dan tune I remember playing was "Chain Lightning." The bassline was fun to play, clean, sharp and set the mood of the tune.

Little Big Band with Donald Fagen, Walter Becker,
Phoebe Snow, and me. Photo by Bonnie Brooks

Donald offered up a remembrance of that time for this book. "At Hades, I knew of Harvey Brooks. He had quite a reputation as a player after 1965 when he played with Bob Dylan. I knew he played with guys like Paul Griffin, Mike Bloomfield and Paul Harris. I remember that he played bass on a session I was on in New York City in the late 60s, but I can't remember the artist. At one point, I remember he picked up a guitar and played this great raggy blues. But at the time, I was just a kid starting out and I was too scared to say hi."

In the summer of 1992, Fagen and his wife, Libby Titus, decided to take the revue on tour. By this time, Donald had been jamming with The Little Big Band for a year. This is when, once again, band drama raised its angry head. As word of the upcoming gig got out, there was a movement to fire me that started with Gary Gold. In his past, I had played an important role in helping him turn his junkie life around.

Gary's story line, as I understood it, was that I was a slow reader and would hinder rehearsals, so I should be fired. The bassist, Zev Katz, should replace me. Gary called Libby, who was producing the tour, to make his move. It backfired.

I got a call at home in Westport from Libby telling me that Gary suggested they fire me. The end result was Kevin Bents, the keyboardist, and I got hired for the Rock & Soul Revue. Of my hiring, Fagen recalled that he hired me for the tour "because I knew Harvey understood the sort of music we were playing. He's a rock, but also very musical."

The tour started in August with rehearsals in Manhattan from Aug. 8 through 11. The lineup included the principal players, plus Phoebe Snow, Michael McDonald, Boz Scaggs, Chuck Jackson and a 10-piece backup band. We were to play 13 concerts. The first show was at the Riverport Amphitheatre (now the Verizon Wireless Amphitheatre) in St. Louis on August 13 and the last at the Pine Knob Music Theatre (now the DTE Energy Music Theatre) in Clarkston, Michigan on August 30.

Donald is an excellent bandleader, who kept everyone interested and involved in playing the music as a tight unit. Walter Becker was the other guitar player and every time we played a Steely Dan tune that he normally played bass on, he'd give me this look. I took it as a complement. The drummer, Leroy Clouden, was terrific and we had a natural lock together.

The tour ended and I was home in Westport. Bonnie had just finished a producing job with the client, Clairol, with her own company, Take 2 Entertainment. The event for Clairol was at Peter Max's studio in Manhattan. There, Bonnie had worked with the model, Patti Hanson, who is Keith Richard's wife. Bonnie and Patti hit it off. She was impressed that Patti had brought her daughters along for the shoot. Bonnie later discovered that she and Patti shared mutual friendships with Jade Hobson, Tricia Kenney and Amy Kalafa.

On projects she produced, Bonnie would often rent Amy Kalafa's editing equipment for offline editing at our home. She and Amy became friends and both families became socially connected through the love of music. Amy and her husband, Alex, were long time friends of Keith and Patti's.

One Friday night, Bonnie got a call from Amy inviting both of us up to their home for a drink. Bonnie said I was at a gig in Hartford, so she would have to pass. Amy then told her to come anyway, since Keith Richards was there and wanted to meet her. So, Bonnie drove up to meet him. When I got home, Bonnie told me about her meeting with Keith. He had kissed her hand and treated her like royalty, saying that he was a fan of mine.

The following morning, Bonnie and I got up early, checked out the yard sale ads in the *Westport News* and took off for our traditional Saturday morning hunt for hidden treasures. As we were coming down Old Saugatuck Road to one of the sales, we saw a jeep rolling out of a driveway and heading toward the river. It stopped before hitting the water. When we walked into the sale, Bonnie asked if anyone owned the wayward jeep. A guy in dark glasses and a funky hat moved toward us, letting us know it was his.

Bonnie immediately recognized him as Keith Richards, who put his finger over his lips, signaling for her not to "out him." That was my first introduction to Keith Richards.

Alex and Amy love to cook and know how to entertain their friends. Alex is from France, and his choice of wine, food and conversation created an ongoing Saturday night soiree that included tasty, whipped conversations. They had a warm French country dining table with benches. This became a regular get together that included Bonnie and I with the Fraboni and Richards families. With wine flowing, we all would share our crazy stories as the different courses arrived. Some of the dinners included roadkill, that had us counting how many legs the so-called chickens had!

The Rekooperators

In 1994, my musical compadre, Al Kooper, hired me to play on his album, *Rekooperation*. In preparation, we did several gigs to get our groove together. Al's vocals and the arrangements were true to their original sources. Once the album was released on the Music Masters label, we did a tour to promote the recording. Unfortunately, the audience just didn't buy into the album.

Al's autobiography, *Backstage Passes & Backstabbing Bastards: Memoirs of a Rock 'N' Roll Survivor*, qualified him as a member of the Rock Bottom Remainders, a loosely affiliated rock band made up of authors that included Dave Barry, Stephen King, Amy Tan, Barbara Kingsolver, Matt Groening and perhaps 10 other writers. The Rekooperators shared the bill with the opening act for the Remainders at the Bottom Line in New York City.

My stepdaughter, Celia, was a big fan of Stephen King's writing and wanted to meet him. She drove all the way from Ithaca College to meet us at the club in Greenwich Village. The Rock Bottom

Remainders tour bus was parked in front of the club. So, after getting the thumbs up from Stephen King, I introduced Celia to Stephen. She then jumped in and deluged him with fan statements and questions, which he graciously answered, while signing the book she had brought.

Shortly after the release of the *Rekooperators* album, Al then put together what I think was one of his best musical projects. It combined works from his previous bands into a single album. These included The Blues Project, Blood, Sweat & Tears (or actually, Child is Father to the Man, since he couldn't use the BS&T name) and The Rekooperators. The project was called Soul of a Man. Al is a great songwriter and producer and can be an excellent performer. On this album project, all of these qualities came together.

As you know, Al and I were childhood friends and our working relationship goes back to high school. Since those early days, we've had an ongoing dispute over how I got paid. He has never included me in the equity of his projects. Al always insists I'm a hired gun. In the album, *Super Session*, for example, I got a tune on the album called "Harvey's Tune," but I was not a principal artist or a writer on the group jams. Needless to say, Al does not agree with my assessment of the business.

The new album was being designed to look like *Super Session* with the photos being laid out in a similar way. My photo would be used for promotion and marketing. Though I was a featured performer, I was considered by Al to be a sideman. Al was happy to use my name with my picture for publicity, yet I was not considered a partner who shared in any of the possible royalty opportunities. He never offered it to me. Had he done so I would not have been so concerned about my fee per gig.

Slo Leak

Bonnie and I were introduced to Danny and Maggie Kortchmar by Terry and Gail Coen, who had recently become their neighbors. Danny is a well-known guitarist who plays with James Taylor's band, as well as a songwriter and producer. He had moved to Westport from Los Angeles but had grown up in New York City and had been longtime friends with Carole King, Carly Simon and James Taylor. We became social friends.

Shortly after our meeting, Danny hired me to play bass on The Fabulous Thunderbirds' *Roll of the Dice* album. After the recording, I was invited to become a member of Slo Leak, his band. This time, I would be an equal partner.

Business difficulties and politics were already present before I came into the band. The original backer of Slo Leak was suing the band for signing a deal with Pure Records. At the time, Steve Rosenfeld was our manager. When the band had label issues, Steve stepped in to help us get a better record deal. He set up showcases for the band with several labels. One was interested but did not want guitarist Charlie Karp as the lead vocalist.

February 12, 1997

Harvey Brooks
P.O. Box 536
Bronxville, NY 10708

Dear Harvey:

Thank you for all of your assistance on the 53rd Presidential Inaugural. Bringing together countless Americans, it was a magnificent celebration of our great national journey.

Your efforts made a real contribution to the success of the Inaugural, and I am grateful to you.

Please accept this special edition of my inaugural Address and a copy of Miller Williams' *Of History and Hope* as small tokens of my appreciation. I hope you enjoy them.

Sincerely,

Bill Clinton

Letter from President Clinton

I wanted to keep Charlie. Danny, however, brought in Babi Floyd, who had played and recorded with Keith Richards and X-Pensive Winos. The move, however, did not get us a record deal. Before the band hit bottom, we did have a major swan song. With Steve's and Bonnie's connections, Slo Leak played at Bill Clinton's second inauguration on February 12, 1997. The band went to Washington, D.C. in a limo from Westport with Steve Rosenfeld at the helm.

Our Clear Channel radio executive friend, Scott Bacherman, interviewed the band during the trip to Washington, D.C. When we hit the metropolitan Washington area, the streets had become one giant parking lot.

Rosenfeld — through sheer adrenaline — shot out of the limo and did his magic, forcing drivers to get out of our way. He enlisted traffic cops to help us get through. He got the band to the inauguration on time and we were ready to play by the time the Clintons walked on stage. The new President crossed in front of us, said a few words and left as we played.

Back home, I got another call from Al Kooper and Jimmy Vivino. They wanted to hire me for a featured gig at the Bottom Line. Steve Rosenfeld was now my manager, so I asked him to call Al to negotiate my fee. I had no idea what the rest of the band was getting, but I knew if I was not going to be a partner in the band that I wanted to be paid more.

Bonnie tried to talk me out of having Steve make the call and to negotiate with Al. She felt we had grown up together and I should call him personally to talk it out. I didn't listen to her. Bonnie, of course, was right. Al blew a gasket and fired me. With my name up on the marquee at the Bottom Line and the gig the following week, I got a call from Jimmy saying that Al had cooled down. I was rehired. I told Jimmy I would pass, since Bonnie and I were leaving for Tucson the following week. Jimmy suggested that I reconsider, but for me I already had a bad taste.

Several years ago, after my move to Israel, I got a scalding email from Al. He said Jimmy did not offer me the bass chair on the *Conan O'Brian Show* because I had passed on the Bottom Line gig. Al said he never wanted to talk to me again. He remains hostile to this day.

With the girls on their own after college, Bonnie thought it was a good time to sell her house in Westport and move into Manhattan, which she thought would make life easier for both of us. We checked apartments and found one on 99th Street and Columbus Avenue. We were downsizing from a suburban four-bedroom house with a pair of cats and dogs to a city apartment with two small bedrooms.

We were about to sign the lease, but something was nagging at me. To delay, I suggested to Bonnie that we have lunch before signing. As we were walking along Columbus Avenue to lunch, we saw a woman being carried out of a building on a stretcher. I took it as some kind of omen. At lunch, I suggested an alternative idea to Bonnie. What if we moved out of town — go on an adventure to somewhere entirely new? It was a totally spontaneous thought, but Bonnie eventually agreed and bought into my idea.

Bonnie's youngest daughter, Julie, suggested we consider Tucson, Arizona. She told us that Tucson was an arty town and affordable. It was only a one-hour flight to Los Angeles. As fate would have it, Bonnie's cousins — Sid and Faye Morse — already lived in Tucson. They invited us to come out and stay with them while we checked out the area.

We accepted their invite while we looked the place over. The Morse's home was located in the North West Tucson foothills. Adjacent to it was a hangar for their plane with a private runway. Upon arrival, we took Sid's aerial tour of Tucson, while he quizzed us on the five C's of Arizona — copper, cattle, cotton, citrus and climate. We were immediately hooked on the area.

By the time our short visit was over, we had rented a house on the North West side of Tucson on three acres surrounded by horse ranches. We learned quickly that our new neighbors included rattlesnakes, coyotes, mountain lions, owls and about 100 fruit bats that occupied the back terrace. The bats would take off every evening after sunset!

Before we left Connecticut, I told Danny and Charlie that Bonnie and I were moving to Tucson, but I was still into the band. With current technology, I suggested, we could record long distance and I could fly in whenever necessary or whenever something was real. We were already three or four tunes into the next album, and I had recorded some bass parts.

About a month or so after we moved, I got a call from Charlie Karp saying that both he and Danny had decided to go on without me since I wasn't local anymore. They did, however, use some of my bass parts from the 1998 session, without my permission, for the *New Century Blues* album. I guess my check is still in the mail.

CHAPTER 22

Bringing Music with You — Wherever You Are

1998: Frank Sinatra dies of a heart attack at age 82.

In Tucson, I was looking to play with folks who could perform my original music. Bonnie mentioned that a woman in her yoga class knew a drummer that I might want to check out. I did. He and I connected musically and we added his friend, guitarist Tom Kusian, who by day owned a food market downtown. We began rehearsing weekly and stepped out to play a few gigs at the Congress Hotel, a local music venue.

Tom was aware that Bonnie and I were savvy with online marketing and suggested that we get together to talk about promoting his market on 17th Street to a larger audience. At that time, the market was called Tucson Fruit and Produce. He hired us both to create his online presence as well as for Bonnie to do the market's public relations and advertising.

When we started, the warehouse had no real color and was a bit rough around the edges. But it had a hometown, authentic feel that allowed us to build on the concept. Bonnie renamed it the 17th Street Market. It was housed in the downtown warehouse district of Armory Park, right next to the railroad tracks. It was a bit difficult to find, which added to its charm.

*Richie Havens at the Katrina Fund benefit for New Orleans organised by Bonnie
Brooks with the help of Tom Kusian and Frank Sanzo. L to R Bonnie Brooks,
Frank Sanzo, Klondike Kohler, Richie Havens and myself.*

Though it was often 110 degrees outside in the Arizona heat, the market was able to stay relatively cool within the huge, sprawling warehouse space. People kept coming, and we and the market kept expanding. We added a large selection of music CDs that included jazz, rock, pop and world music. Because customers began to buy the CDs, and at Bonnie's and my urging, Tom dedicated an area of the market to create a music store. As an additional enticement for me, Tom built a studio for playing and recording music next to our offices.

We also added sections to promote local artists, Chinese herbs and housewares. Bonnie started to bring in local musical artists to play at the 17th Street Market on Saturdays. Her first big event was with my old friend Richie Havens, who performed at a benefit for the Katrina flood victims of New Orleans. All proceeds for the sold-out concert were donated to The Katrina Piano Fund.

To the folks of Tucson, it was mind-blowing to see a guy who had played at Woodstock performing in a local Tucson warehouse. That was just the warm effect we wanted.

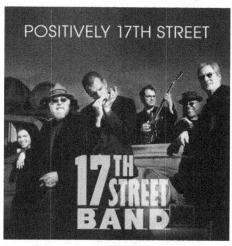

As the music shop grew, we added musical instruments, the "Carl Hanni Vinyl Road Show," where poet, music critic, blogger and collector Carl Hanni would set up his record collection and play, buy, sell and trade vinyl rec-

L to R Arthur Migliazza, me, Tom Walbank, Dustin Busch and Darryl Roles

ords, the Chris Larson 17th Street Market Luthier Show and regular Friday drumming circles.

The market became a daytime hub for food, art and music. The owners of the market gave Bonnie a lot of support and encouragement to build up their business. Their sales and notoriety had increased dramatically. With more international foods on the market's shelves, we added the additional spice of world artists that were appearing at The University of Arizona.

One was Alhaji Papa Susso, a kora virtuoso, traditional musician and oral historian who descended from a long line of griots in Gambia, West Africa. I noted that the kora is a difficult instrument to play and Papa Susso shared his knowledge and talents with me at the market music store. It was a wonderful event.

While working at the market, Bonnie and I recorded and

produced two albums for 17th Street Records, our label, which we co-owned with Tom Kusian. One was *Positively 17th Street* by the 17th Street Band, a group Bonnie and I had put together. The other was *The Gift/El Regalo* by Francisco Gonzalez, the original co-founder of Los Lobos. He is an amazing multi-instrumentalist and vocal artist who Bonnie recruited when Francisco was shopping at the 17th Street Market's fish counter.

Scott Barker, our friend who is the executive editor of *Tucson Lifestyle*, a local publication, recalled visiting with us at the ware-house.

"I walked through the store, down by the seafood section and through this little corridor," Barker recalled. "Inside, were crates of old record albums and there they were, Bonnie and Harvey, in these two old dinky offices. "It just struck me at the time as I went there that here is this world-class musician — a rock icon — in the back of a warehouse in Tucson. It was surreal, but at the same time it made sense, because this was an organic place, and I don't mean just in terms of gardening. It was homegrown very much like a commune atmosphere from the 1960s."

Barker noted that we were surrounded by music. "Music to Harvey was clearly the stuff of life. Just as much as bread or anything else. The guy just lived, breathed and ate music.

"Harvey was the most mellow, humble guy I can think of. There are people in Tucson that are very impressed with themselves and are great self promoters. But that wasn't Harvey at all. He was just a guy. Bonnie talked up his accomplishments more than he ever did. To talk with Harvey, you would never know what he had accomplished and who he had played with.

"He was like Babe Ruth when he retired from baseball. Ruth still played with small leagues and random games because he deeply loved the game. Harvey was the same way. He loved music and has kept playing it because it is deep inside him."

When Bonnie and I started working at the market, the economy was booming. When the housing bubble burst in 2008, the reality of maintaining a music recording business and world food market faded. There was a distribution deal with City Hall Records, but no budget for promotion.

At a partner meeting — on the back steps of our office that overlooked the market's parking lot — Bonnie brought up her concern for our future. She felt that the record label and our situation at the market were not going to move any further and it would be wise for us to check out other opportunities. It was a very difficult decision for Bonnie to make since her youngest daughter, Julie, and her family lived in Tucson and they were very close. Celia and her family were in Ithaca, New York and Lori, Bonnie's oldest daughter and the mother of nine, lived in Israel.

Bonnie suggested two possibilities; one was to move to San Francisco where she knew she could work in public relations. Or we could take — as she called it — "a leap of faith" and move to Israel to be closer to Bonnie's older daughter, Lori. There, I would be able to branch out into the music market of Europe. I opted for her leap of faith in Israel and my life has not been the same since.

Israel had never been on my radar, so living there had never crossed my mind. Bonnie's love for the land of Israel had been part of her life since her junior year in high school when she visited for a summer. My initial trip to Israel was when Bonnie was still in treatment.

Julie had hit her junior year in high school and Bonnie thought it would be a positive experience for her to spend a year at Kibbutz Beit HaShita in northern Israel. When Julie had some trouble adjusting to kibbutz life, Bonnie booked us on a flight to see what was going on. This was my first trip to Israel.

When we got to the kibbutz, Julie told us she had been fired from her job on the olive inspecting line. She was accused of allowing pits in some of the olives to pass her at the conveyer belt. Her story was hilarious, and it reminded me of the famous episode of *I Love Lucy* with Lucy and Ethel eating chocolates on an assembly line. Julie's was the pits!

Julie was much happier once she was moved to cleaning the zoo at the kibbutz, which at least included a camel. I laughed and loved the whole experience!

We met wonderful people in Tucson that will be in our lives forever. As we packed up to leave, we spent quality time wishing all goodbyes. On our departure day, Pete Wagner, who oversaw the 17th Street Market, picked us up to make our flight. We had heavy luggage plus two dogs — a Pekinese and a Chihuahua in one carry case — and our Siamese cat in another. Bonnie and I owe Pete for his warm friendship and guidance during our time in Tucson. At the airport, we unloaded our life's belongings and Pete drove off.

The beginning of our leap included the classic financial beating of being over-charged by Delta Airlines for our oversized bags and our carry-on pets. As we were gagging dollars, we suddenly heard the melodic sound of a Mexican harp. To our amazement and joy, there was our friend Francisco Gonzalez, master musician, playing us forward into our new journey.

Before leaving Tucson, we had talked to Tom about our partnership in 17th Street Records. It would continue without our presence. We felt that we could promote the label from a distance and came to a fair mutual agreement. Six months after our arrival in Jerusalem, we got a phone call from Tom, telling us that the 17th Street Market would no longer be funding the record label and that Tucson Food Services would take over the ownership. I guess it was to be expected. Eventually, the entire 17th Street Market closed, citing its inability to be competitive. We personally thought they had made a big mistake, but it was fun while it lasted.

Our first days in Jerusalem could be called *Jerusalem for Dummies!* We had not done any research or long-term planning and it was showing. We have since learned how to put down roots in a country that has a different language and culture. Now, we understand what it's like to be an immigrant in the United States.

We found ourselves learning not to expect call backs from anyone, but to go and meet people in person to let them know what we needed. This helped get our electrical service installed, our medical care established and to make daily life easier on the street.

We do not have a car and use mass transportation to move around the city. We've learned that Israelis do not queue well and how to hold our place in a line. We've climbed Masada, floated in the Dead Sea and swam at the beach in Tel Aviv.

We've shopped the Jewish and Arab markets in Jerusalem and know where to find the best dates, bakeries and produce. I've played the best clubs and recorded in excellent Israeli studios. On the Jewish high holidays, we pray at the Western Wall and have taken friends to visit the Al-Aqsa Mosque. We began by living in one area of Jerusalem, moved to another and then to another — feeling like true Bedouins. Today our home is in the Abu Tur neighborhood and we love it. The great leap of faith worked out well for us.

CHAPTER 23

Meeting the Greats

Willie Dixon

When I was living in Los Angeles working on an ill fated resurrection of The Electric Flag, I got a call from bass player/trombonist Lui Lui Satterfield, formerly of Earth, Wind & Fire, saying I should get singer David "Lefty" Foster to drive us up to Glendale, California, in his Cadillac to get some songs for the new Flag album from the songwriting legend Willie Dixon. Lui Lui knew Willie from Chess records in Chicago where Lui played bass on Fontella Bass' "Rescue Me." As Lefty drove, Lui Lui was navigating and I was in the back seat with my eyes closed listening to Willie and Memphis Slim in Paris perform "Baby Won't You Please Come Home" on the car's cassette player.

I passed a joint over to Lui, as we talked about stuff that Willie played on or wrote. We were all caught up with the enthusiasm of Willie's contributions to the music that we all loved and played. There were few songwriters of his status and I was excited to be able to meet him.

Willie Dixon played on many of the great hits by Chuck Berry, Bo Diddley, Little Walter and Howlin' Wolf. What I knew — from hearing Muddy Waters perform "Hoochie Coochie Man" and Mose Allison sing "Seventh Son" — is that so many great blues songs that I heard or had seen performed by both black and white artists had been written by Willie Dixon.

As we pulled into the driveway of the Dixon's three-bedroom home, Lui Lui told me that Willie bought his house in 1982 with royalties he won back in court from Led Zeppelin. Willie had to sue them for stealing the lyrics for "Whole Lotta Love" from his 1962 song "You Need Love."

We knocked on the door and were greeted by Willie himself. He gave Lui a hug and me and Lefty a polite nod. He was a big man — tall and wide. As he led us through his living room to his den, I noticed a baby grand piano sitting in the middle of the room with sheet music and pages of lyrics strewn across the top. To me, those were signs of a compulsive songwriter.

Once in the den, Willie sat back in his recliner lounge chair and lit up a joint and passed it over to me. I knew that Willie had been a boxer in his youth, just like Miles Davis. He was the Illinois Golden Gloves Champion. I asked him why he gave up boxing. His answer revealed his sly sense of humor: "I gave it up when I realized I could make more money playing music without being beaten to a pulp. "

I was sitting across from a living legend who has written more than 500 songs — many of them million sellers. He was one of the most important songwriters who ever lived and appealed to both black and white audiences. We were there for three hours listening to tunes which included Willie's tune, "It Don't Make Sense (You Can't Make Peace)" on his cassette player.

The lyric:

You have made great planes to scan the skies,
You gave sight to the blind with other men's eyes,
You even made submarines stay submerged for weeks,
But it don't make sense you can't make peace.

When Willie's grandson came running into the den jumping onto grandpa's lap, we knew it was time to go. As we left, Willie gave me a cassette, some sheet music, some lyrics and these words of advice: "When you tell the story, be true to yourself. Make it believable and make sure your business is straight." These were words that apply as much to life itself as to music.

From our conversations about songwriting and life, I could sense Willie's bitterness brought on by having to live on survival money due to Chess Records cheating him out of his publishing royalties. It took him years to get back what he was owed, causing needless financial difficulties and frustrations leading to his poor health.

As we pulled out of Willie's driveway, Lui Lui put on Willie's 1970 album, *I Am the Blues*, as we settled back for our ride home. It was a joy to get a personal glimpse into the life of a songwriting legend.

Otis Blackwell

I was hanging out at Jim and Andy's Bar on 48th Street just west of Sixth Avenue in Manhattan, a 1960s haunt for musicians between recording sessions. While there, I got a call from my answering service saying there were some upcoming demo sessions with Otis Blackwell and was I interested in working on them. I asked how much it paid and was told $50 a tune with a three-song guarantee for a three-hour session beginning at 5 p.m. The next day. I took the gig.

I knew Otis Blackwell only by reputation. He had written "Don't Be Cruel" and "All Shook Up" for Elvis Presley as well as "Great Balls of Fire" and "Breathless" for Jerry Lee Lewis. He also wrote "Fever," recorded by Little Willie John and Peggy Lee. He was one of the greatest R&B songwriters of all time. His songwriting style is as uniquely identifiable as that of Willie Dixon, Chuck Berry or

Leiber and Stoller. He helped redefine popular music in America in the 1950s.

When I got to the studio, Otis was running down his song list of hits with a drummer, piano player and background singer. I saw quickly that Otis was actually auditioning players for some local New York gigs and trying out some new tunes he was working on. When I arrived, he looked at me and asked, "You the bass player?" I answered, "Yeah."

The studio engineer then directed me to my amplifier and chair and wired me up. Otis said, "You come highly recommended, let's get to it." He counted off "All Shook Up." That was the beginning of a two-month New York City interboro tour — one that led to my playing and partying with the man who wrote some of R&B's most iconic songs. I was with Otis at one of his favorite spots, a dance club in Brooklyn, where he had a grand old time playing his hits.

Since Otis was born in Brooklyn, he knew all the neighborhood people and by the end of the night so did I. In between sets before meeting up with his old friends — we would talk about songwriting. "It's all in the title of the song," he said. "Pay attention to what's going on around you, cause that's where the story comes from. It could be the shaking of a soda pop bottle, that's where 'All Shook Up' came from."

I asked Otis how he got into music. He said he won a local talent contest at the Apollo Theatre in Harlem in 1952 and got a recording contract with Joe Davis' Jay-Dee label. It was at Davis' suggestion that he began writing his own songs. "I was thrown into it," he told me.

Otis said he would hear something that caught his ear or see something that caught his eye and would write it down. He would never pre-judge what he was observing...he would just write it down. It was interesting because Dylan did the same thing, taking notes with friends as he walked down New York City streets. It's as if great songwriters harvest thoughts and snippets of information from the environment all around them.

Otis asked if I wrote, and I said I did. He asked if he could hear some of my tunes. I played him "Harvey's Tune" from the *Super Session* album and "What a Wonderful Thing We Have" from The Fabulous Rhinestones. I just happened to have it on my Sony Walkman at the time. He nodded with a smile and then played me some new demos he had just finished. They were from that demo rehearsal session we had done.

Hanging out with Otis Blackwell was like going to a school that specialized in humanity. Though he had been through years of dirty publishing tricks and manager-writer royalty scams, Otis was not a bitter man. I asked, "Doesn't it bother you that they stole your money over the years?"

His response: "Yes, but there was still enough for me take care of my family and live comfortably. I don't want to spend time and money making lawyers rich. I spend my time writing songs."

Otis Blackwell taught me to keep my eyes on what is really important in life and to not get sidetracked by negative, destructive issues.

B.B. King

"The guy that I think has done more for blues than most people, which is why we called him the Godfather, was Muddy Waters. So when Muddy Waters went to Chicago, Chicago opened its arms and let him in. Then a lot of the young people, and especially young white people, started to listen to Muddy Waters. Muddy Waters is the guy to me who did it." — B.B. King

My introduction to B.B. King's music took place after winning a dance contest when I was 16 years old in Queens. The prize was a record album called *The Blues* by B.B. King. After hearing this album, I bought myself a Harmony Monterey F-hole guitar with the money I earned from my Long Island Daily Press paper route and played along with King.

I was first introduced to B.B. King himself at Bill Graham's Fillmore Auditorium in San Francisco in 1967 on a split bill featuring The Byrds, The Electric Flag and B.B. King. Mike Bloomfield was a disciple of B.B.'s and he introduced me to him as the bass player of the Flag.

B.B. asked if Mike was working me hard to keep that pocket simple and solid. I had never thought about what I was doing in those terms. B.B. took the abstract action of my playing and gave me a lesson of good blues bass playing in one short sentence.

In 1974, The Fabulous Rhinestones were on tour promoting our third and final album. We were in Atlanta, Georgia at the Agora Ballroom opening up for B.B. King. I hadn't spoken to him since the Fillmore gig and I was looking forward to re-introducing myself and swapping stories.

The dressing rooms for the artists as I recall were below stage right, one staircase down. As usual, Mr. King's valet had already set up his dressing room. The band was sitting around, warming up and getting ready to go on just as Mr. King entered the dressing room with a beautiful woman on his right arm and his guitar, Lucille, in the left.

B.B. asked me how Bloomfield was and what had happened to the Flag. He was not surprised to hear that because of drug problems, the band folded. We started talking about a musician's life on the road and what it takes to survive and be successful. He had the formula down cold, while I was still figuring it out.

I asked him what made him start off at the beginning of his career with a 10- or 12-piece band. He said he needed the support because he wasn't very good with chords. He built his whole sound based on a call and response pattern like used at church. Singing a line, then answering with a guitar lick and then having the band play chords. He knew exactly what he was doing.

The last time we shared a stage together was with The Alligator All Stars' half-hour set that was on the menu in 1993 at Hard Rock Café in New York City. B.B. King, Lonnie Brooks, Junior Wells and Buddy Guy joined this dynamic group. I played bass, Jeff Levine was on the Hammond B3 organ and Jack Scarangella played drums. What a night!

Left to right: Me, Lonnie Brooks, Buddy Guy, Jack Scarangella and Junior Wells at B.B. King's Blues Club in Manhattan. Photo by Bonnie Brooks.

CHAPTER 24

My Thoughts and Discoveries on the Electric Bass

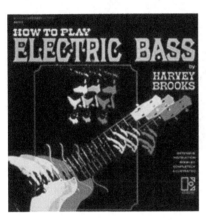

In 1967, I was invited to do an instructional album for the electric bass guitar on Elektra Records. I worked with artist manager Arthur Gorson to come up with my teaching concept. At the time, I was already recording and performing with Eric Andersen, Tom Rush, David Blue and Jim & Jean. Arthur had pitched Jac Holzman at Elektra Records on the idea of Bob Dylan's electric bass player doing an instructional album on the instrument. Holzman liked the idea and we were in business.

Gorson hired recording engineer Bill Szymczyk to co-produce this album with me. We called the project *How to Play the Electric Bass*. Bill, later in his career, went on to become the producer of The Eagles, The James Gang, B.B. King, Joe Walsh and many others. This was the first production project for both of us. My good friend Paul Harris and I wrote the 20-page instructional booklet that was included in the final release.

Now — more than a half century later — I find myself writing down what I've learned and absorbed from other musicians through the years. The knowledge I have picked up comes in various forms and in numerous ways. It is often heard just while killing time between sessions with other musicians in the studio.

Over time, I have learned that a solid and confident bassline requires many factors. These include:

- Notes played to their full values. The articulation of a note is sustained until the next note begins.
- Building strength in the left hand, with exercises designed to give the fingers control of holding and sustaining individual notes.
- Dedication — playing every day builds strength and makes the hands stronger.
- Use of rhythm and harmony that supports the melody, creating a cushion for the melody to sit on.
- Support the basic rhythm figure of the song that is provided by a drummer's bass drum, the rhythm guitar and the piano part.
- Musical fills that introduce the next chord change.

All the theory I've learned has come from on-the-job training and a desire to create and communicate with other musicians.

Here are my Ten Commandments of basic bass playing:

1. Tune up
2. Learn the form and chord changes of a piece of music by creating your own chord chart or use round and round or over and over repetition method to learn parts.
3. Create your part by syncing or playing off the drummer's bass drum pattern.

4. Get your basic rhythm figure from the combined rhythmic figure being played by all instruments.
5. Listen to the high hat for the rhythmic feel, quarter note, eighth note or sixteenth note.
6. Learn the Cycle of Fourths – C-F-Bb-Eb-Ab-Db-Gb-B-E-A-D-G. This works going up four steps. Example: C-D-E-F going up to F or down five steps C-B-A-G-F going down to F.
7. Know the basic major and minor scale formulas – The major *WS=Whole step *HS=Half step.....WS,WS, HS,WS,WS,WS,HS - The minor scale formula — WS,HS, WS,WS,WS,HS,WS.
8. When creating a bass part, start with the root and fifth of the key you're in. As you get comfortable with the tune begin building the part, selectively using notes in the scale of the key you're in.
9. Play along with songs you like and learn the bass parts by ear.
10. Always play with musicians that challenge you.

I find that most musicians — when learning to read notes after they've started playing chords and "Stairway to Heaven" — have trouble playing along with a metronome. The metronome helps to develop the math of music. It becomes much easier to play quarter, eighth and 16th notes when time is consistent.

The tendency is to rush, lag or eventually totally ignore it. My suggestion is to react to the click rather than anticipate it. Play each note's full value, changing to the next note as soon as the click is heard. A sense of timing is the clock of life. It never speeds up or slows down. The metronome helps internalize a sense of time that allows a musician to have the freedom to play around the beat, to humanize the music.

As a sideman — whether creating a part in a rhythm section or being part of an orchestra — I always begin by opening up my bag of tried and true tricks to get myself comfortable, so I can make everyone around me comfortable. I check out the chart for any difficult passages or markings. If there is no chord chart or arrangement, I write out the song form. Example: AABACABB. A=Verse, B=Chorus, C=bridge, then the chord progression that fills each section. I then connect the sections during the rundown. When the rundown of the tune includes the melody — whether vocal or instrumental — that's when I have enough musical info to play my best bassline.

I remember being in-between sessions waiting in the lounge at the Hit Factory in New York City one day when Bob Babbitt, the great Motown bass player, also between sessions, came in to take a break. We started talking about how we get our sounds, because that's what bass players do. Babbitt showed me his bass. It was a Fender Precision with the pickups flat to the body and a piece of foam just touching the strings up against the bridge. He liked his sound to be percussive with no overtones. All of his great recordings, like Stevie Wonder's "Signed, Sealed, Delivered I'm Yours" and Marvin Gaye's "Inner City Blues," use that same pickup and foam arrangement. It is during moments like this that musicians learn from others.

My favorite recorded bass lines include: "Summer Breeze" by Seals and Crofts, "Touch Me" by The Doors, "Season of the Witch" on *Super Session*, "Ballad of a Thin Man" by Bob Dylan and "Great Expectations" on Miles Davis' *Bitches Brew*.

CHAPTER 25

What It All Comes Down To

Great talents, I believe, emerge from some psychic cage from which the artist perpetually seeks escape, or which he or she feels may once again serve as their residence. We run toward art as we flee the circumstances that made it possible.

It is not enough to be angry, but I believe that all art arises from a foundation of rage and regret. The artist is lucky in that he finds the means to sing or write or dance or build or teach; the untalented angry find an art in cruelty or destruction, and the world, I am afraid, is a perpetual battle between these two teams of abused and frightened and confused people, and we are either saved by the artists or destroyed by the miscreants.

That, my dear, is show business. That is life.

—James Grissom

Throughout most of my life, I've been a loner. Like a gypsy nomad always on the move, I never stayed anywhere long enough to put down roots. There were many girlfriends, houses, jobs, projects, bands and gigs along the way. I lived in places like New York City,

Mill Valley, Woodstock, Atlanta, Hollywood, Sag Harbor and Queens. Everywhere I went in my younger years, music was my true companion in life.

But music is not the same as loving, laughing or doing battle with my wife Bonnie, my life partner. Though Bonnie and I come from the same neighborhood, we speak a different language. Her love for her family is first and foremost and her sense of values are irrefutable. Me, never having had children or roots, added a very different spin to her life. She has made me whole. We have been together for 31 years.

Two years ago we lost our youngest daughter, Elizabeth Julie. It is not easy to share or explain just how difficult this has been for all of our family. But life is fragile, and we all learn to live it one day at a time and not take anything or anyone for granted.

So, what have I learned from my years of being a musician?

The first 26 years of my career in music was dictated by extraordinary opportunity and my reaction to it.

Being a musician, for me was about the music and nothing else. Throughout my lifetime, I have had to overcome not adversity, but my own adverse stupidity. In 1967, when I joined The Electric Flag, I started smoking pot and drinking alcohol. Though I was able to take advantage of the opportunities given me, eventually the drugs and alcohol started to wear on me physically and spiritually.

My love of music sustained me until I started to get sloppy due to the drugs. In spite of myself, I survived the times, which is more than I can say for many of my friends. Along the way, however, I made a lot of questionable decisions that set me back professionally. As I see it, when drugs and alcohol figure into a project, the end result is usually doomed to failure. It may take awhile, but the world will crash and burn around you.

The important thing to remember is that music is also a business — an often brutal one. As Van Morrison once said, music is spiritual, but the music business is not.

———

I love to play music. But as a player, I never paid much attention to the business side of music. I never insisted on contracts because I didn't want to rock the boat. This was due to my own insecurities. I just wanted to get the gig and play the music I loved. I learned the hard way that without signed agreements or contracts, you become the last in line to get paid when there is trouble.

When you leave important decisions in your life to other people, you take on the responsibility for their mistakes — whether intentional or not. Musicians like Billy Joel and Leonard Cohen are good examples of successful artists who let other people handle their business affairs and ended up having to go to court to try to recover lost money. Getting advice from lawyers, managers and business consultants can be helpful, but at the end of the day the musician has to make his own decisions and live with those choices.

In the creation of music, technology keeps changing. In the end, it does not matter. What truly matters is the artistry of musicianship. Musicianship is as timeless as human existence itself.

I have always tried to bring artfulness to my work, to be creative and engage the music with my heart. When playing, I don't think about the technical issues. I listen and react. I'm in the moment and play my groove.

At the time of this writing, I am 76 years old. I have had the good fortune to play with many stellar musicians and have shared my music and talents with audiences all over the world. My move to Israel with the incredible Bonnie has opened up a new source of influence to my musical vocabulary.

Life is a complex experience. I have stood up when I should have sat down and sat down when I should have stood up. Whatever the results of my actions are, I add them to my vocabulary of life and continue the journey.

The story of life
Is quicker than
The wink of an eye
The story of love
Is Hello and Good-by
Until we meet again

Jimi Hendrix

Marriage

The important element was that someone believed in me
and felt that I was her star.

Our beginning – St. Croix

MUSEUM OF ART, SCIENCE & INDUSTRY
4450 Park Avenue, Bridgeport, CT 06604

Rock & Roll: Art & Artifacts
March 11 — May 14, 1989

Shake, Rattle & Rock.
Join the artists and musicians at the opening reception
Saturday, March 11, 1989
8:00 — 11:00 p.m.

Rock Art by Keith Haring, Ritchie Havens, Annie Leibovitz, John Lennon, Robert Mapplethorpe, Peter Max, Michael McCartney, Andy Warhol and others.

Artifacts of Meatloaf, Jim Morrison, Elvis Presley, Neil Sedaka and others.

Good Vibrations and Libations

RSVP
Members $15, Guests $20
Supporting Members and above free

This exhibition made possible with the support of the Connecticut Commission on the Arts, a State Agency whose funds are recommended by the Governor and appropriated by the State Legislature

William L. Haney, "On—Rock Around the Clock",
Oil on canvas, 54" x 72", 1988, Courtesy Sherry French Gallery, NYC

Flyer for Bonnie's show.

HAIL, HAIL ROCK AND ROLL

The Museum of Art, Science and Industry braces for a celebration of 30 years of musical history

Westport's Meatloaf kicks out the jams. His jacket will be in the MASI show.

The Mar Of the I

He's been labelled a m
A look at the voting re
Speaker Richard Baldu

By Lesley Riva

Now that the dust has settled around the
center, anche of former
Stage Speaker Irving
Stolberg, witnesses are
turning new attention
at the man who has
replaced him—and why
want new alliances is
said every news of reg-
relation and twenty-three years

Richard Baldus, who
have near veteran of the
largely an opinionary result
genius, somewhere in the
accompanied his succession
"moderate"—not as liberal
as conservative as the P
put him in power might

But does the label fit?
Action Group, a 70,000-
organization, gives the n
50 percent on its legisla
voted with the organizat
sumer, labor, environme
issues, only 50 percent
in 1974. "That 50 perce
bottom fifth of all sitting
bly," says Ethan Rome
speaker Stolberg, in co
of 91 percent.

In the 1986 and 198
issues such as worker

BY JIM MOTAVALLI

Art and rock and roll are such natural friends it's a wonder they don't get together more often. Both draw on their creators' most spontaneous inspirations, and both are rich reflections of the culture of their time. But anarchic rock has never been a comfortable visitor to the socially stratified, New York-based art world, and that's what makes the upcoming show at the multi-leveled Museum of Art, Science and Industry (MASI) so special. It's one of

Newspaper article about Bonnie's show.

First dance.

Sister Bert, Bonnie, Me, My Mom Fay, Brother Gary

Brother Morey, Bonnie, Bonnie's Father Martin, Mom Irene and
Brother Lloyd.

Julie and me – Photo by Bonnie Brooks.

Ziv Bar Ilan, Creator of Zoybar Guitar.

Invited for dinner at our home in Tucson. Nick (the chickens dry, after showing up late) Gravenites 2007. Photo by Bonnie Brooks.

Phoebe & me, 1992. Photo by Bonnie Brooks.

Phoebe Snow, Cyndi Lauper, Donald Fagen Little Big Band at the
Bearsville Theater in Woodstock. Photo by Bonnie Brooks.

Al Kooper and me at the Bottom Line in NYC.
Photo by Bonnie Brooks.

Jimmy, Al, and me. Photo by Bonnie Brooks.

Michael McDonald and me. Photo by Bonnie Brooks.

Portrait by Bonnie Brooks.

New Music Project

I have played and created many different styles of music through my career. My new project reflects those influences as well as the contributions of the musicians who accompany me on this journey.

I am in the process of recording my own project which has been my dream. My band mates are Oren Fried, Yehuda Ashash, Steve Peskoff, Ioram Linker and Jamie Saft.

I would like to thank Ehud Banai & Danny Sanderson, well known Israeli Artists, for sharing their talents with me.

Danny Sanderson and me. Photo by Bonnie Brooks.

Me, Ehud Banai and Yehuda Ashash.

Me and Jamie Saft. Photo by Bonnie Brooks.

Afterword

On the recent loss of our daughter Julie, we would like to thank the special angels who watched over us through this difficult time. Faye Morse, Tamara and Gerald Bush and family, Paulette and Larry Crawshaw, The Hamani family, Doug and Jen Bartlett, Lee Brandt, Daniel Crawford, Paula Sepulveda and the whole Crawford family.

We wish to thank Debbie Carroll at MusiCares for her sympathetic ear and MusiCares for their financial assistance in helping us to cover some of Julie's expenses, including her rent for her first year of her treatment.

The Recording Academy's charity, MusiCares, provides a safety net of critical assistance for music people in times of need. MusiCares' services and resources cover a wide range of financial, medical and personal emergencies, and each case is treated with integrity and confidentiality. MusiCares also focuses the resources and attention of the music industry on human service issues that directly impact the health and welfare of the music community.

We lovingly thank all the friends, family and strangers that supported the fund that Julie's beloved sister Celia put together through youcaring.com

Elizabeth Julie Brooks

Loving Mother of Isabelle, Ariana, Eli and Adam

March 24, 1976

April 10, 2018

Appendix

Harvey Brooks-Discography

1. Bob Dylan – *Highway 61 Revisited* – Columbia – 1965
   a. Single – "Positively 4th Street"

2. Tom Rush – *Take a Little Walk with Me* – Elektra – 1966

3. Eric Andersen – *That's Alright Mama* – Vanguard – 1966

4. David Blue – *David Blue* – Elektra – 1966

5. Jim & Jean – *Changes* – Verve Folkways – 1966

6. Harvey Brooks – *How to Play Electric Bass* – Elektra – 1967

7. The Electric Flag – *The Trip: Original Motion Picture Soundtrack* – Sidewalk – 1967

8. Ian & Sylvia – *Lovin' Sound* – MGM – 1967

9. Peter, Paul and Mary – *Album 1700* – Warner Bros. – 1967
   a. Single: "I Dig Rock and Roll Music"

10. Eric Andersen – *'Bout Changes 'N Things* – Vanguard – 1967

11. Mike Bloomfield, Stephen Stills, Al Kooper – *Super Session* – Columbia – 1968

12. Richie Havens – *Mixed Bag* – Verve Forecast – 1968

13. Mama Cass – *Dream a Little Dream* – ABC/Dunhill – 1968

14. The Electric Flag – *A Long Time Comin'* – Columbia – 1968

15. The Electric Flag – *An American Music Band* – Columbia – 1968

16. Freakout – *You Are What You Eat* (Original Soundtrack) – Columbia Masterworks – 1968

17. Hedge and Donna – *All the Friendly Colours* – Capitol Records – 1969

18. Eric Mercury – *Electric Black Man* – AVCO Embassy – 1969

19. Sonuvagun – *Last Summer* (Original Motion Picture Soundtrack) – Warner Bros./Seven Arts – 1969

20. The Doors – *The Soft Parade* – Elektra – 1969
    a. Singles – "Touch Me," "Wishful Sinful," "Tell All the People"

21. Tony Kosinec – *Processes* – Columbia – 1969

22. Karen Dalton – *So Hard to Tell Who's Going to Love You the Best* – Capitol Records – 1969

23. Kathy McCord – *Kathy McCord* – CTI Records – 1970

24. John and Beverley Martyn – *Stormbringer* – Island Records – 1970

25. John Sebastian – *John B. Sebastian* – Reprise – 1970

26. Starship – Paul Kantner – *Blows Against the Empire* – RCA Victor – 1970

27. Miles Davis – *Bitches Brew* – Columbia – 1970

28. Bob Dylan – *New Morning* – Columbia – 1970
    a. Single – "If Not for You"

29. John Cale – *Vintage Violence* – Columbia – 1970

30. Bobby Lester – *Bobby Lester* – Columbia – 1970

31. Seals and Crofts – *Down Home* – T-A Records – 1970

32. John Hall – *Action* – Columbia – 1970

33. Al Kooper – *Brand New Day* – Landlords soundtrack – Columbia Records – 1971

34. John Simon – *John Simon's Album* – Warner Bros. – 1971

35. Pacheco and Alexander – *Pacheco and Alexander* – Columbia – 1971

36. Seals and Crofts – *Summer Breeze* – Warner Bros. – 1971
    a. Singles: "Summer Breeze" and "Hummingbird"

37. Fabulous Rhinestones – *The Fabulous Rhinestones* – Just Sunshine Records – 1972

38. Fabulous Rhinestones – *Freewheelin* – Just Sunshine Records – 1973

39. John Compton – *To Luna* – Ageless Records – 1973

40. Rosalie Sorrels – *Whatever Happened to the Girl That Was* – Paramount Records – 1973

41. Rachel Faro – *Refugees* – RCA Victor – 1974

42. Miles Davis – *Big Fun* – Columbia – 1974

43. The Rhinestones – *The Rhinestones* – 20th Century Records – 1975

44. Loudon Wainwright III – *Unrequited* – CBS –1975

45. Al Kooper – *Anthology/Al's Big Deal/Unclaimed Freight* – Columbia – 1975

46. Gilles Rivard – *Impulsions* – Sonogram – 1975

47. Leo's Sunship – *We Need Each Other* – Lyons Record Co. Inc. – 1978

48. Miles Davis – *Circle in the Round* – Columbia – 1979

49. Tony Wilson – *Catch One* – Bearsville – 1979

50. Jerome Olds – *You Lift Me Up* – Heartstring – 1980

51. Miles Davis – *Un Enigma Da Musica Negro-Americana* – Abril Cultuural – 1980

52. The Doors – *Greatest Hits* – Elektra – 1980

53. Michael Bloomfield – *Bloomfield: A Retrospective* – Columbia – 1983

54. Electric Flag – *The Best of the Electric Flag* – Back-Trac Records, CBS Special Products – 1984

55. Miles Davis – *A Portrait of Miles Davis* – CBS – 1987

56. Jimi Hendrix – *Café Au Go Go Jam Session* – Koiné Records – 1988

57. Jimi Hendrix – *Jammin' With Friends* – Koiné Records – 1989

58. Miles Davis – *The Columbia Years 1955-1985* – Columbia – 1988

59. Miles Davis – *Volume 3* – Columbia – 1981

60. Bob Dylan – *The Bootleg Series Volumes 1-3 (Rare & Unreleased) 1961-1991* – Columbia – 1991

61. John Sebastian – *Tar Beach* – Shanachie Records – 1992

62. Neal Black and the Healers – *Neal Black and the Healers* – DixieFrog – 1993

63. Al Kooper – *Rekooperation* – MusicMasters – 1994

64. Michael Bloomfield – *Don't Say That I Ain't Your Man! – Essential Blues 1964-1969* – Legacy, Col. – 1994

65. John Cale – *Seducing Down the Door–A Collection 1970–1990* – Rhino – 1994

66. Miles Davis – *Le Meilleur De Miles Davis* – Columbia – 1994

67. The Fabulous Thunderbirds – *Roll of the Dice* – Private Music – 1995

68. Fontella Bass – *No Ways Tired* – Nonsuch – 1995

69. John Simon – *Harmony Farm* – Pioneer – 1995

70. Peter Green Songbook – Viceroy Music Europe – 1995

71. Al Kooper – *Soul of a Man* – MusicMasters – 1995

72. Groovy: A Collection of Rare Jazzy Club Tracks – 1996

73. Bob Dylan – *The Best of Bob Dylan* – Sony Music TV/Columbia – 1997

74. Paul Burlison – *Train Kept a-Rollin'* – Sweetish Records – 1997

75. Miles Davis – *The Complete Bitches Brew Sessions* – Columbia Legacy – 1998

76. Bob Dylan – *From Newport to the Ancient Empty Street in LA* – Dandelion – 1998

77. Tom Rush – *The Very Best of Tom Rush* – Columbia Legacy/Common Chord – 1999

78. The Doors – *The Complete Studio Recordings* – Elektra – 1999

79. Paul Pena – *New Train* – Hybrid Recordings – 2000

80. Ken Burns Jazz – *The Story of America's Music* – Columbia Legacy – 2000

81. Miles Davis – *The Essential Miles Davis* – Columbia Legacy – 2001

82. Raisins in the Sun – *Raisins in the Sun* – Rounder – 2001

83. Miles Davis – *The Best of Miles Davis* – Columbia Legacy – 2002

84. Bob Dylan – *No Direction Home: The Soundtrack* – Columbia Classic Records – 2005

85. Various Artists: *Sous Les Paves*, LeJazz – Sony BMG Music/Columbia Legacy – 2008

86. Various Artists: *The All New Electric Muse Album* – Universal Music/Operations Limited – 2008

87. The 17th Street Band – *Positively 17th Street* – 17th Street Records – 2009

88. Francisco Gonzalez – *The Gift* – 17th Street Records – 2009

89. Bob Dylan – *The Original Mono Recordings* – Columbia – 2010

90. Richie Havens – *Mixed Bag/Something Else Again* – Raven Records – 2010

91. The Doors – *A Collection* (6-CD Set) – Elektra/Rhino Records – Doors Music Co. – 2011

92. Rob Paparozzi – *The Ed Palermo Big Band* – Electric Butter – 2014

93. Bob Dylan – *Bob Dylan's 50th Anniversary Collection 1965* – Columbia Legacy – 2015

94. Bob Dylan – *The Best of the Cutting Edge 1965-1966* – Columbia Legacy – 2015

95. The Electric Flag – *The Electric Flag Featuring Erma Franklin/Live 1968* – Rockbeat Records – 2015

96. Betty Davis – *The Columbia Years 1968-69* – Light in the Attic – Columbia – 2016

Also of Interest, by Bonnie Brooks

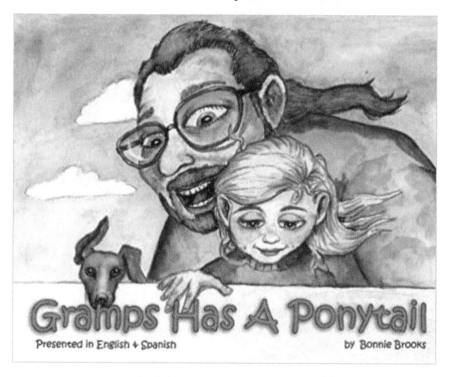

Gramps Has A Ponytail. This is a fun adventure of Sam spending the day with her Gramps, who happens to be the notorious bassist Harvey Brooks. Harvey has accompanied the likes of Bob Dylan, Jimi Hendrix, The Doors, Seals and Croft, Miles Davis, Judy Collins, Richie Havens, Janis Joplin and Cass Elliot to name a few. This enduring story takes place in New York, is fully illustrated and includes English and Spanish in one book.

Other books from Tangible Press

Blown Out on the Trail
20 Years of Unreleased Bob Dylan Recordings

Nominated for the 2020 Association for Recorded Sound Collections Awards for Excellence in Historical Recorded Sound Research. *Blown Out on the Trail* is the second in a series of books dealing with the unreleased recordings of Bob Dylan.

Skipping Reels of Rhyme
A Guide to Rare and Unreleased Bob Dylan Recordings

Nominated for the 2019 Association for Recorded Sound Collections Awards for Excellence in Historical Recorded Sound Research. In 1994, the first comprehensive website devoted to the works of Bob Dylan was created. This book presents some of the original articles written for the site, concentrating on the unreleased tapes of Bob Dylan, with commentary on the merits of each tape.

The Thylacine's Lair
a novel by Graham Parker

Originally published by Thunder's Mouth Press under the title *The Other Life of Brian*, this out-of-print novel by Graham Parker is being republished under its original title, *The Thylacine's Lair*.

The Songs of Squeezing Out Sparks
40th Anniversary Edition
Compiled by Martin Belmont

40th anniversary edition. All the lyrics, chords, bars, tablature and notation of lead guitar, including solos plus extracts from the rhythm guitar. Some songs with both guitar tabs in their entirety. Acoustic guitar picking intro of You Can't Be Too Strong. Includes extracts from reviews, adverts, plus live and promo photos from publications such as Rolling Stone, New Musical Express, The Village Voice, and much more.

Visit http://tangiblepress.net for the complete catalog

Made in United States
Orlando, FL
20 November 2022

24787511R00157